W9-CNN-827

WHEN FASHION REALLY WORKS

A Quintessence Book

This edition for the United States and Canada published in 2013
by Barron's Educational Series, Inc.

All inquiries should be addressed to:
Barron's Educational Series, Inc.
250 Wireless Boulevard
Hauppauge, New York 11788
www.barronseduc.com

ISBN: 978-1-4380-0342-9

Library of Congress Control No. 2013930077

This book was designed and produced by
Quintessence Editions Ltd.
230 City Road, London, EC1V 2TT

Editor	Becky Gee
Designer	Tom Howey
Editorial Director	Jane Laing
Publisher	Mark Fletcher

Color separation by KHL Chromagraphics, Singapore
Printed by 1010 Printing International Limited, China

9 8 7 6 5 4 3 2 1

FRONT COVER:
Magical Fashion, from *Harper's Bazaar* (December 2008)
© Richard Burbridge / Art + Commerce

BACK COVER:
Jean Paul Gaultier, Couture Collection Fall/Winter 2012/13

Marnie Fogg

WHEN FASHION REALLY WORKS

BARRON'S

CONTENTS

EXOTICISM

ASCETICISM

SUBVERSION

REVIVALISM

THEATRICAL

FUTURISM

INTRODUCTION

At its most powerful, fashion epitomizes and illuminates the attitudes of an era, shaping a generation and defining cultural changes and divisions. As an industry, it drives and responds to innovative technology; it is also subject to the forces of a changing global economy. Great fashion requires a dedicated audience—whether an upscale couture clientele or an urban avant-garde—and must satisfy the needs of a sophisticated fashion retail system. When it articulates a new paradigm for style, transfiguring the norm with an expressive potency, great fashion attains covetable status and everlasting importance.

When Fashion Really Works documents the many and varied aspects of fashion at its most compelling, influential, and directional, and provides a unique collection of a century's most enduring styles. It identifies eighty outstanding garments from the beginning of the twentieth century, when the fashion system as we know it was fixed firmly in place, to the present day. Each is incorporated into a themed chapter—Luxury, Form, Exoticism, Asceticism, Subversion, Utility, Eroticism, Revivalism, Theatrical, and Futurism—and more precisely identified by a subsidiary theme that captures the essence of the piece. For example, an evening ensemble designed by Parisian couturière Madeleine Vionnet features in the Form chapter and is explored in terms of the sculptural qualities inherent in the draping and cutting of cloth.

Le Bar Suit (1947)
Dior
⊠ FORM p.37

PREVIOUS PAGE: Bias-cut Evening Ensemble (1931) **Vionnet**
⊠ FORM p.35

The book examines why certain garments develop from one-season statements into fashion classics, remaining immutable throughout the vagaries of seasonal change and becoming permanent fixtures in the fashion firmament. The simplicity of the tweed cardigan jacket and A-line skirt introduced by Chanel in 1954 provided an antidote to the wasp-waisted look established by Dior's "New Look" in 1947, but continues to constitute a contemporary fashion exemplar. Each selected item is significant for different reasons. These range from the appropriation of other cultures, as seen in Lanvin's exotic *robe de style* in the 1920s, to the radical transposition of proscribed elements, such as the use of underwear as outerwear by Jean Paul Gaultier for his conical bra dress in 1984. Some garments mark an overnight change of silhouette, from Dior's New Look to the adoption of the "sack" dress—a full-backed, waistless chemise devised by Givenchy and Balenciaga in 1957—which led to the development of the 1960s shift dress. Others are evidence of a cerebral approach, such as the slashed robes of Rei Kawakubo for Commes des Garçons, which were initially labeled "Hiroshima chic" by the fashion press in the 1980s, but were still adopted by an army of fashion and media aficionados.

The fashion world has a long-standing relationship with luxury, and the luxury heirloom remains a contemporary preoccupation, whether designed

Feather Dress (2011)
Sarah Burton for Alexander McQueen
» LUXURY p.29

and produced by heritage labels, such as Hermès, or by modern, fresh talent, such as British designer Mary Katrantzou. Luxury now resides in the extreme refinement not only of the bespoke and the exclusive, but also of the idiosyncratic and the unusual, as seen in Sarah Burton's deployment of the art of the plumassier in her feathered ball gown for Alexander McQueen in 2011. The allure of the exotic also remains an ever-present theme in fashion. This is evidenced in the primal appeal of reptile and animal skins, exemplified by the patterned excesses of Italian designer Roberto Cavalli, and the desire for rich embellishment and quirkily proportioned lavish textiles seen in the 2012 collection designed by Marc Jacobs, celebrating the nineteenth-century origins of luxury label Louis Vuitton.

In contrast, the restrained minimalism of ascetic dress is usually epitomized by masterful tailoring, bereft of any extraneous detail. The appeal of an austere white shirt or the clean lines of a trouser suit by Jil Sander, pioneer of 1990s understatement, provides a simplicity that remains modern and directional, seen in the pared-down play on scale by Phoebe Philo at Céline. In the twenty-first century, minimalism is softer around the edges, with designers such as Martin Margiela adding texture from unfinished edges and delicate lace to the purity of the unadorned form. In some instances, the fashion show, held in one of the

Planet Gaia (2010)
Vivienne Westwood
» REVIVALISM p.155

four major fashion capitals—New York, London, Paris, and Milan—provides an environment in which to challenge preconceived notions of beauty and glamour: in 1997, distraught and disheveled models staggered down the runway in shredded clothes to show Alexander McQueen's "Highland Rape" collection. Social and political concerns may also be manifest in the appropriation of both text and images: witness Vivienne Westwood's polemic on global warming and her defense of Planet Gaia.

The provenance of a garment is not always the responsibility of a designated designer. This is particularly true of those items that come under the heading "Utility." The trench coat was designed initially in 1914 for the soldiers of World War I, but has been reworked in diverse textiles, such as suede and duchesse satin, to become a timeless favorite. Similarly, the fishtail parka was first worn by the U.S. army in 1951 to help the soldiers cope with freezing conditions during the Korean War, and was later appropriated by the mod subculture in the 1960s. Today the garment is a transseasonal must-have, a staple item produced by mass-market manufacturers and high-end designers. British designer Stella McCartney popularized the jumpsuit—originally a tough all-in-one that provided protective cover for industrial workers—and in 2012 finessed it in luxurious fabrics with flights of fancy embellishment. Denim jeans

Leotard (1985)
Donna Karan
⯮ UTILITY p.115

have also acquired a designer price tag and are offered with variations of cut (bootleg, skinny, boyfriend, cropped) and finish (distressed, stonewashed, dyed, printed.) However, they remain true to their origins—hard-wearing and easy to launder—and always feature a front fly, double-stitching, and rear pockets.

The introduction of active and spectator sportswear was generated by the increasing importance placed on the role of health and fitness in the late nineteenth and early twentieth centuries. This was consolidated by the burgeoning popularity of mass travel and tourism. Breaking the boundaries of appropriate wear, women adopted relaxed, all-in-one beach pajamas in the 1920s. These were first worn over a swimsuit, before evolving into loungewear—for example, wide-legged, palazzo pants worn for informal occasions inside the home set the precedent for integrating sportswear into fashion. The same trend precipitated easy-to-wear, one-piece dressing, when Donna Karan reinterpreted the dancer's leotard for the businesswomen of the 1980s, who adopted it as functional daywear, worn in the office beneath fuss-free wrap skirts and over black opaque tights.

When Fashion Really Works also reveals the relationship between fashion and eroticism, differentiating between the sensuality of Mariano Fortuny's Delphos pleated silk gown and the overt sexuality of the bikini in the era of

Tea Dress (2013)
Tomas Maier for Bottega Veneta
» REVIVALISM p.157

the mid-century pin-up. Fetish wear was introduced to mainstream fashion in the 1990s by designers such as Alexander McQueen and Vivienne Westwood, and proved to be one of the most significant styles of the decade, prompting the debate as to whether the constraints of the corset were degrading or empowering for women.

Fashion continually refers back to both the recent and the distant past. It is constantly reacting to the contemporary norm and is inevitably preoccupied with the new. Historical revivalism remains a fixed theme in fashionable dress, exemplified by Tomas Maier's reinterpretation of the 1940s floral printed tea dress for Italian luxury house Bottega Veneta in 2013. His exquisite interpretation of past modes is in contrast to the ironic pastiche of garments such as the Union Jack jacket from I Was Lord Kitchener's Valet. The mannered attitude of "romanticism," finding expression in the resurrection of historical ideas, even extends to an engagement with the cultural and atmospheric values of former periods. Revivalism would be meaningless without these invisible connections.

The relationship between fashion and the theatrical experience is inextricably linked, from the hard-edged suiting of Hollywood designer Adrian for the power-driven, postwar businesswoman, epitomized by film actress Joan Crawford, to the influence of Spanish flamenco on the boldly ruffled skirt

Structured Top and Skirt (2013)
Alexander Wang
FUTURISM p.193

by Nicolas Ghesquière for Balenciaga. As a fashion subculture, the gothic accoutrements of lace and leather, first seen on the stage of the Grand Guignol theater, continue to provide a dark form of glamour.

The future of fashion is often predicated on the assumption that life will be lived differently. In truth, futuristic fashion is less to do with the introduction of new materials and techniques and more to do with a visionary concept of the role of clothes, epitomized by Japanese designer and textile innovator Issey Miyake. His polychromatic flying saucer dress remains a one-off, whereas John Bates's mesh-banded mini is as wearable today as it was in the 1960s. Modern futurism also means the skillfully drawn lines of Alexander Wang's lambskin skirt and top, in which fragments of fabric float over the surface of the body suspended by invisible filament in what may be seen as a homage to the 1960s space-age fashions of Paco Rabanne and what was then a new acceptance of nudity, transparency, and brevity. This caused avant-garde U.S. designer Rudi Gernreich to note, "Clothes are disappearing."

Of course, they never did.

LUXURY

"The greatest and most celebrated proponent of the engineered gown is Charles James, widely regarded as America's greatest couturier. He developed his own methodology based on mathematical, architectural, and sculptural concepts as they related to the human body."

Patricia Mears
fashion writer

The use of black lace heightens the drama of the white duchesse satin.

Four-Leaf Clover Ball Gown 1953

Charles James

Luxury is not confined to the use of expensive materials; it is also defined by limited accessibility. Charles James created only a small body of work, chiefly produced between 1947 and 1954, partly because of his meticulous and time-consuming working methods. He also refused many commissions, and sometimes left garments incomplete or failed to meet important deadlines. However, the United States' fashionable elite commissioned his engineered gowns for the grandest occasions. The four-leaf clover dress is constructed from white duchesse satin and ivory silk faille with an overlay of black velours de Lyon around the hem and the waist. It consists of four layers: an inner taffeta slip, a structured underpetticoat, a matching petticoat flare, and an overdress. The garment is constructed from thirty pattern pieces, twenty-eight of which are cut in duplicate, the remaining two singly.

Modeled on the Victorian prototype of the crinoline, the four-leaf clover gown created a true fashion spectacle. The skirt stands a great distance away from the body, rendering the wearer inaccessible and creating a space around her for an appreciative audience. Denying her both comfort and mobility—she was unable to sit down or dance—the bodice of the dress has a rigid boned understructure, and the skirt is balanced on the waist to support and distribute its great weight.

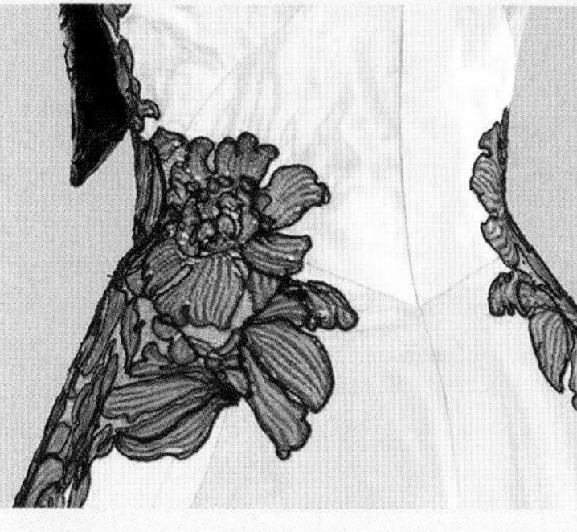

Ball gown
Jean-Philippe Worth
1898

Junon evening dress
Dior
1949–50

Infanta gown
Ralph Rucci
2004

Propaganda dress
Vivienne Westwood
2005–06

Wedding Dress of Princess Grace 1956

Helen Rose

The formal wedding ceremony is collectively regarded as an occasion on which no expense is spared, when the all-important dress is made from the most luxurious of materials and fashioned into the most traditional of styles. The all-white wedding dress, popularized by Queen Victoria in 1840, is seen here worn by Hollywood royalty: internationally acclaimed film star Grace Kelly on her marriage to Prince Rainier of Monaco in 1956. Helen Rose designed the dress, which was made from 25 yards (23 m) of eau de soie, a heavyweight smooth satin, together with 98 yards (90 m) of tulle, 25 yards (23 m) of silk taffeta, and 300 yards (275 m) of antique Valencienne lace.

The veil and train are significant for their symbolic role. The veil represents Hymen, the god of marriage. Obscuring the face during the ceremony, it is lifted only after the vows have been exchanged. Kelly's veil is embellished with appliquéd lace lovebirds and thousands of seed pearls. The Juliet cap is also decorated with seed pearls and orange blossoms, which are a Mediterranean symbol of fertility. The length of the train is an established element of court dress, denoting the wealth and status of the bride's family: the more formal the ceremony, the longer the train.

The full-skirted crinoline with fitted bodice is the template for the traditional wedding dress.

Court presentation ensemble
Boué Soeurs
1928

Elizabeth II's coronation gown
Norman Hartnell 1953

Catherine Middleton's wedding gown
Sarah Burton 2012

Pop Art Print Dress 1991

Versace

Attesting to his own predilection for exuberant excess and in keeping with the conspicuous consumption of the era, Versace provides layer upon layer of embellishment in this Pop art print gown. The print registration of each color—primarily yellow, emerald green, red, cerulean blue, purple, and gold—is deliberately inaccurate, resulting in an overlap of slightly mismatched color. Armfuls of polychromatic and gilt bangles and chandelier earrings add to the impression of unrestrained excess.

In homage to the pop culture of the 1960s and the vibrantly colored screen prints of celebrities by U.S. artist Andy Warhol, Gianni Versace fashioned an allover print featuring portraits of Hollywood's most enduring style icons—sex goddess Marilyn Monroe and screen idol James Dean—into a clinging, ankle-length evening dress. The artfully constructed showgirl-style bustier top projects the breasts outward and upward, the embonpoint emphasized by luxurious scrolls of rhinestones and appliquéd motifs created by attaching extra pieces of material to wire supports. These form curvilinear patterns around the breasts before outlining the plunging "V"-shape of the neckline at the center front and back.

"The Versace customer does not wrestle with implications of moral philosophy; she flirts and dazzles and gives men a hard time."

Nicholas Coleridge
president of Condé Nast International

Versace's raunchy sensuality is captured by supermodel Naomi Campbell.

Palmyre evening gown
Dior
1952

Evening ensemble
Yves Saint Laurent
1980

Primarily the creator of totemic handbags, an outward symbol or emblem of conspicuous luxury, Hermès diversified from its equestrian roots with a couture collection in 1929. The company continued to engage its long-held specialist skills in the use of leather, and worked various animal and reptile skins into timeless fashion collectibles of butter-soft suede trenches and crocodile-skin jackets under the creative direction of various designers, including Belgian designer Martin Margiela. In this ensemble by Jean Paul Gaultier for the label, the distinctive Hermès signature burnt orange of the leather is fashioned into an oversized wrap shearling coat. It is accompanied by the natural tones of luxurious noble fibers, such as camelhair, cashmere, and silk, the latter featuring a paisley print. Hermès eschews modern processes, such as digital printing, in favor of the more expensive and time-consuming traditional methods of screen printing for its cloth, in which each color—up to forty—requires a separate screen.

This shearling wrap coat, bordered and lined in fur, offers a subtle statement of luxury and wealth.

Orange Suede and Paisley Ensemble 2008

Hermès

"The world is divided into two: those who know how to use tools, and those who do not. We will continue to make things the way the grandfathers of our grandfathers did."

Jean-Louis Dumas
Hermès artistic director

Creating heirlooms for the next generation involves designing highly desirable products that accrue rather than relinquish their value over the years. Timelessness, meticulous craftsmanship, and the eschewing of short-lived trends all contribute to the longevity of a classic design and ensure its appeal to future generations. Although Hermès is one of many luxury brands, it differs from others in that it remains a family-run business, currently in the hands of a sixth generation. The company does not use celebrities to market its products and it does not license its name. Not overtly conspicuous, it is an example of "stealth wealth."

Leather greatcoat
Alexander McQueen
2003

Silver python tuxedo
Armani Privé
2008

Hand-crocheted biker jacket
Christopher Kane with Johnstons of Elgin 2011

Tweed tulle embroidered skirt suit
Karl Lagerfeld for Chanel
2012

Jewel Tree Dress 2011
Mary Katrantzou

Lavish complexity and spectacular graphic opulence have placed the collections of British-based Mary Katrantzou at the hub of media attention each season since her launch in 2009. The high degree of finesse—digital and manual—that she deploys in the realization of the form, patterned imagery, and surfaces of her garments creates a sense of playful conspicuous consumption, with an undercurrent of the permanence of the heirloom. She engineers intricate placement prints that feature precious, exquisite objects, such as Coromandel screens, Fabergé eggs, Qianlong dynasty china, and Meissen porcelain, and contains them within her strict signature silhouette.

Embellishment of any sort extends an artifact beyond its core functionality into the realms of enhanced values. Katrantzou luxuriates in creating extreme textiles from different sources that interplay between hyper-real *trompe l'oeil* effects and extravagant, real embroideries. The designer harnesses digitally engineered patterning and additional handwork to reinforce three-dimensional garment form. The appliquéd tulip skirt reads as a semi-rigid structure, and the richly printed panné velvet bodice, with an inset peplum, creates a sultry undergrowth of stylized flora and fauna.

The Jewel Tree dress is heavily encrusted with crystals, beads, and three-dimensional roses.

Silk evening dress
House of Worth
1892

Tweed jacket and gold lace tutu
Versace
1992

Byzantine dress
Alexander McQueen
2010

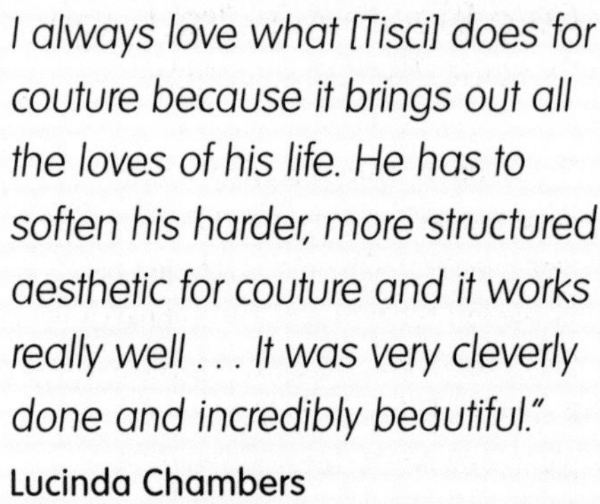

I always love what [Tisci] does for couture because it brings out all the loves of his life. He has to soften his harder, more structured aesthetic for couture and it works really well . . . It was very cleverly done and incredibly beautiful."

Lucinda Chambers
fashion director

A rich abundance of embellishment provides high-impact glamour and photographic opportunities on the red carpet.

Cate Blanchett's Dress 2011

Riccardo Tisci for Givenchy

The luxuriant embellishment and exquisite technique seen in Cate Blanchett's gown were combined by Riccardo Tisci in homage to kabuki and the art of Butoh. The samurai armor-inspired biblike breast plate is left plain but painstakingly outlined with embroidered layers of bubbling three-dimensional beadwork that features Swarovski crystals and pearls that deepen in color from gray to pale yellow. The hard-edged geometric structure of the bodice and angular sleeves are offset by the soft draping of the skirt, layers of pale lavender silk chiffon tulle falling free from an embellished obi-style belt, and with vertical pockets hidden in the seam.

Representations of women are everywhere in popular culture, and some of the most influential are found in the movie industry. An appearance on the red carpet provides the perfect showcase for a collaboration between an actress and a couturier. This mutually beneficial arrangement ensures invaluable publicity for the label. The celebrity red-carpet gown is photographed from all angles, and therefore demands an interesting back view, seen here in the embellished, crossed straps and squared-off collar, which reveal the back bare to the waist for optimum exposure.

Nicole Kidman's dress
John Galliano for Dior
1997

Julianne Moore's dress
Tom Ford for Yves Saint Laurent Rive Gauche 2003

Halle Berry's dress
Versace
2005

Jennifer Lopez's dress
Jean Dessès
2006

Feather Dress 2011

Sarah Burton for Alexander McQueen

In a formidable demonstration of technical expertise that utilizes all the artisanal skills of the McQueen atelier, the duck feather bodice is molded to imitate the fall of a bird's plumage. The plumassier painstakingly treats dyes and applies the fragile feathers to the garment in a meticulous and highly concentrated process. Hand-stitched overlapping layers of feathers create a high-necked collar, extending over cap sleeves cut in one with the bodice and continuing the line of the shoulders.

Sarah Burton's first collection as head of the label after fourteen years as assistant to Alexander McQueen evidences their shared obsession with research. It comprises a series of luxurious gowns characterized by an ethereal and romantic beauty. In this example, Burton deploys the signature McQueen elongated torso and smothers it in palest lavender feathers. From the plunging waistline, the ostrich feather tendrils of the skirt tremble and sway with the model's movement. The feathered panniers of the skirt create the illusion of wings that are about to open, an image reinforced by the small train at the hem, which gives the appearance of tail feathers.

> *"Lee [McQueen] taught me . . . there's no snobbery in inspiration. It can be something on the telly or something you see in the street or in a book or a museum."*
>
> **Sarah Burton**

The feather evening gown exemplifies the signature hand-crafting of the label.

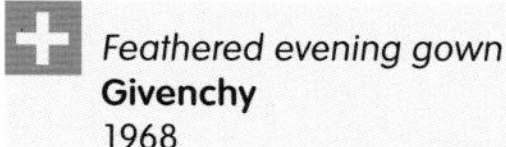

Feathered evening gown
Givenchy
1968

Silk poppy ensemble
Arnold Scaasi
1983

"It was very important to give the essence of femininity, the essence of glamour, and the essence of haute couture—the perfection in the dress. It is like a sculpture that is made on the body of the lady."

Valentino

Valentino's intense color and dramatic simplicity of form create understated glamour on the runway.

Rosso Valentino Evening Dress 2012
Valentino

Since the launch of the Valentino couture house in 1959, Hollywood superstars, queens, princesses, and the fabulously wealthy have taken the opportunity to raise their profile significantly by choosing Valentino. The designer's enduring passion for a specific tone of red—defined culturally and commercially as Rosso Valentino, and chromatically, in additive RGB values, as Red 237, Green 70, and Blue 62—has been an ever-present element in all his collections. With a timeless simplicity that leaves behind the opulent volumes and subtle contrasts of rich fabrics to express both luxury and glamour, this flowing couture gown, from the 2012 collection by Maria Grazia Chiuri and Pierpaolo Piccioli, asserts the core heritage of Valentino. Like the majority of designs produced by the house over five decades, the evening gown offers no challenge to the wearer; it colludes with the figure and her motion to create an aura of female allure.

Offering über-glamour on the runway from the couturier of choice for the red carpet, the Valentino big occasion gown elevates the status of the wearer and fixes the gaze of the onlooker. A dramatic crêpe de chine cape is grown from ankle-length sleeves and allowed to flow backward to the ground in a swirl of sunray pleats. The simplicity of a naturally waisted evening gown is asymmetrically perforated on the bodice by sheer panels of chiffon at the throat and knee.

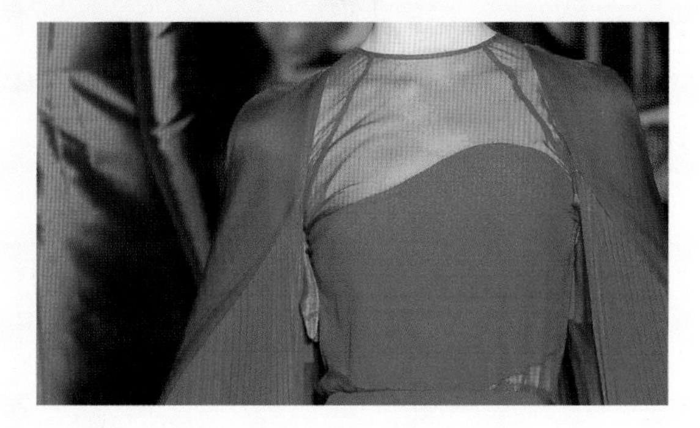

Silk and feather evening dress
Louiseboulanger
1928

Shredded silk chiffon evening dress
Balenciaga 1950

Pink feathered evening gown
Givenchy
1968

Paper taffeta gown
Madame Grès
1969

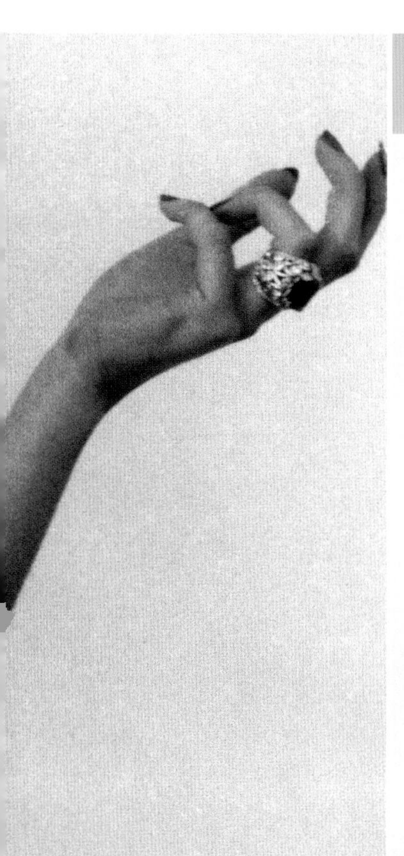

FORM

Bias-cut Evening Ensemble 1931
Vionnet

Inspired by the classical antiquities of the Greeks and Romans, Madeleine Vionnet abandoned corsetry in favor of exploring the potential of draped, wrapped, and folded cloth, as seen in these evening pajamas worn with a matching scarf. She experimented with the Greek chiton, an ankle-length garment cut from a single length of cloth, and incorporated both non-Western and classical techniques of garment construction, based on the loom width of cloth, in her designs. Her methods involved minimal cutting, and she worked with specially commissioned extra wide lengths of material. Generally considered to be the inventor of the "bias cut"—a technique in which the fabric is cut across the grain, rather than along it—the couturière often cut the fabric on the straight of the grain, then turned the pattern pieces so that they draped on the bias; she also utilized Euclidean geometry to create new forms of construction.

Replicating the drapery of classical sculpture with her favorite crêpe de chine and silk chiffon in neutral tones, Vionnet utilized bias-cut ties and panels wrapped around the body to create fit and structure, obviating the need for the traditional bust, waist, and hip darts or fastenings such as buttons or zips. The designer was also inspired by the free-form dance style of her friend and muse Isadora Duncan, who is considered by many to be the founder of contemporary dance.

George Hoyningen-Huene captures the neoclassical lines of Vionnet's bias-cut pajamas.

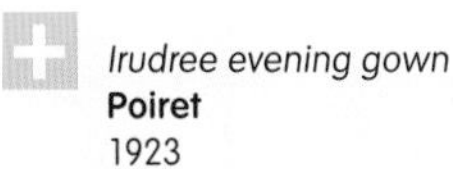

Irudree evening gown
Poiret
1923

Cape and dress ensemble
Jean Patou
1931

Columnar evening dress
Calvin Klein
2011

> *I wanted my dresses to be constructed, molded upon the curves of the feminine body, whose sweep they would stylize. I was creating a completely whole new look, one that the world had never seen before."*
>
> **Christian Dior**

The swirling skirts and narrow waist of the New Look dominate the global fashion scene.

Le Bar Suit 1947
Dior

A new era of luxuriousness was heralded by the introduction of Parisian couturier Christian Dior's radical Corolle line in 1947. It was instantly dubbed the "New Look" by fashion journalists, and it marked the welcome return of the hourglass figure, after a period dominated by the masculine silhouette and uniform-inspired wartime clothes. Dior's commitment to the lavish use of textiles—he was financed by textile manufacturer Marcel Boussac—combined with an adherence to a romantic and nostalgic view of the feminine form resulted in a bold collection that created a furor in the fashion press and spearheaded the postwar revival of Paris as the center of international fashion and the haute couture system. One of the best-selling items of Dior's New Look was Le Bar, a two-piece suit that exaggerated the female form by accentuating the body's curves, thus epitomizing the new femininity.

Dior superimposed an independent sculptural form over the natural lines of the female body by deploying an infrastructure of wire, whalebone, cambric, and taffeta to add volume to the breasts and hips and to constrict the waist. This was enabled by the use of closely woven fabrics such as wool taffeta and duchesse satin. The pale shantung jacket is heavily seamed into the waist, before extending beyond the line of the hips to form a carapace over the pleated, mid-calf, black wool skirt.

Swing coat
Jacques Fath
1940s

Two-piece A-line skirt suit
Chanel
1956

Polka-dot polonaise dress
Christian Lacroix
1987

Balloon skirt
Giambattista Valli
2005

"Perfection is one of the goals I'm seeking. For a dress to survive from one era to the next, it must be marked with an extreme purity. Once one has found something of a personal and unique character, its execution must be exploited and pursued without stopping."

Madame Grès

Madame Grès manipulates the surface of the fabric into a series of intricate tucks and pleats.

Pleated Evening Dress 1955
Madame Grès

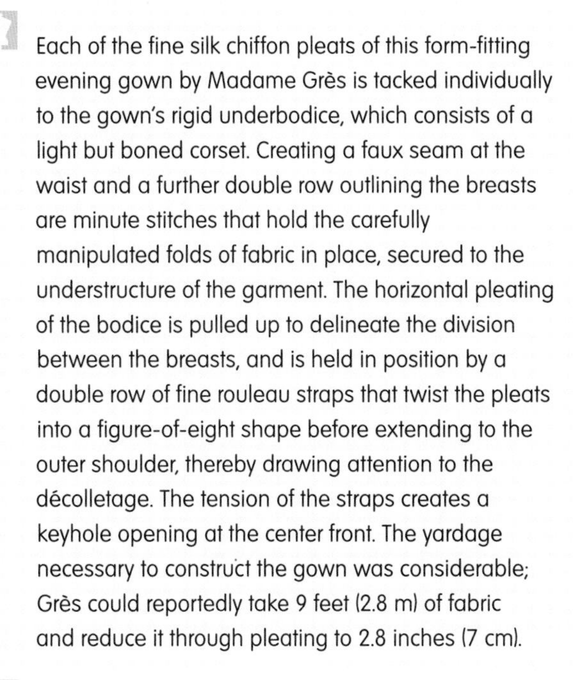

Each of the fine silk chiffon pleats of this form-fitting evening gown by Madame Grès is tacked individually to the gown's rigid underbodice, which consists of a light but boned corset. Creating a faux seam at the waist and a further double row outlining the breasts are minute stitches that hold the carefully manipulated folds of fabric in place, secured to the understructure of the garment. The horizontal pleating of the bodice is pulled up to delineate the division between the breasts, and is held in position by a double row of fine rouleau straps that twist the pleats into a figure-of-eight shape before extending to the outer shoulder, thereby drawing attention to the décolletage. The tension of the straps creates a keyhole opening at the center front. The yardage necessary to construct the gown was considerable; Grès could reportedly take 9 feet (2.8 m) of fabric and reduce it through pleating to 2.8 inches (7 cm).

Referencing Greek mythology and timeless beauty, Grès deploys the fine pleating inherent in fluid classical forms to create the hourglass silhouette and languid femininity of an era defined by its commitment to perfectly groomed glamour. The goddess gown retains a contemporary relevance in its purity of form, use of luxurious fabrics, lack of extraneous decoration, and expert craftsmanship. Grès utilized her signature technique repeatedly to produce variations of the same neoclassical dress.

Draped gown
Travis Banton
1936

Evening ensemble
Schiaparelli
1939

Evening ensemble
Emanuel Ungaro
1990

Diamond drape bodice dress
Isabel Toledo
2005

Skirt Suit 1956
Chanel

The pared-down simplicity of Chanel's easy-to-wear classic suit is due, in part, to the cloth: an unpatterned, textured, hand-loomed wool bouclé, firm enough to hold its shape but providing the ease of wear of a cardigan. The jacket is accessorized with gilt chains and pearls, but has no extraneous decoration apart from a handwoven braid along the edge of the horizontal pockets, cuffs, and center front. The knee-length A-line skirt provides ease of movement and incorporates practical vertical pockets.

Against the prevailing aesthetic of the undulating hourglass figure propounded by Christian Dior, Coco Chanel introduced a timeless two-piece skirt suit that provided the contemporary woman with an elegant uniform to accommodate the demands of modern life. In acknowledgment of the shape of the body, the A-line silhouette neither accentuates nor obscures its form. The jacket is cut to create a narrow torso, emphasized by the high arm scye and narrow sleeve. The braid and gilt buttons do not detract from the simplicity of cut, but are used to define and highlight the structure of the suit. In order to provide consistency of form, the hems of the jacket and skirt are weighted, which ensures an even line.

What a science there is in being well-adorned, what a weapon in beauty, but what elegance there is in understatement."

Coco Chanel

Chanel's classic two-piece skirt suit features an edge-to-edge jacket and A-line skirt.

Trousers and leather tank
Phoebe Philo for Céline
2011

Coat and dress
Jil Sander
2013

“[The sack dress] was inspired by modern art, the experimental art that seeks new shapes and forms, transgressing the limitations set by convention. With my new dress forms, I have discarded the limitations set by the female figure itself.”

Hubert de Givenchy

Modeled by Audrey Hepburn in 1958, the striking simplicity of form of the “sack” dress provides modern ease.

Sack Dress 1957
Givenchy

Providing an alternative silhouette to the hourglass form that had dominated fashion for a decade, Paris-based couturiers Hubert de Givenchy and Cristóbal Balenciaga both produced the "sack" dress in 1957. It set the precedent for the chemise-style dresses that followed, including Mary Quant's youthful minidresses. Givenchy's loose-fitted sleeveless dress barely skims the body and is cut to bypass the waist, before curving in at the hemline (opposite). Although women eagerly adopted this new style, men reputedly disliked the figure-concealing "sack" line, and the dress evolved into the more fitted sheath dress that appeared during the following decade.

As creative director of the House of Balenciaga, French fashion designer Nicolas Ghesquière revisited the label's design archives in 2006 and produced a modern version of the influential sack dress, rendered in heavy radzimir and embossed silk (left). The term "sack" references the pleated eighteenth-century *sacque*, or sack-back, gown, which Balenciaga had revived in the form of the chemise dress with back fullness in 1957. Ghesquière continues the theme by recalling 1960s modernism in the cutaway sleeves and turtleneck, as well as in the purity of the bright white silhouette.

Chemise dress
Dior
1957

Ankle-length sack dress
Simonetta
1958

Rayon crêpe minidress
Mary Quant
1962

Gray/black jersey dress
Zero Maria Cornejo
2009

"When is a dress more than just a dress? When it has magical figure-flattering properties, molds and enhances every sexy curve, and makes the wearer look like a million dollars. It's the reason why some of the world's hottest A-listers, from Demi Moore and Cameron Diaz to Scarlett Johansson, have all walked the red carpet in a Galaxy dress by Roland Mouret."

Grazia magazine

The spectacular and flattering silhouette provided by the Galaxy dress has earned it cult status.

Galaxy Dress 2005
Roland Mouret

Named the "dress of the decade" when it first appeared in 2005, the form-fitting Galaxy dress by Roland Mouret offered a radical return to the hourglass figure, and defined a new era in fashion. Immediately elevated to classic fashion status, the dress became a byword for perfectly shaped femininity and led to a multiplicity of copies. The squared-off shoulder line and the length of the skirt, which falls to just below the knee, evoke a 1940s cinematic feel. The pencil skirt follows the line of the hips and ends in a small fishtail kick. These features help to give the impression of a slim waist, the position of which is slightly above the natural waistline in order to create a longer, leaner torso.

A powerful infrastructure within the lining of the dress suppresses and enhances the contours of the body to create an undulating silhouette. The infrastructure is constructed from Powerflex: a tough, stretchy fabric that previously was used to make underwear during the 1950s. The precise tailoring and the accurate placing of the darts at bust, waist, and hips are further enhanced by the use of wool and stretch felt fabric. The built-on, stand-away shoulder detail of ruched cap sleeves balances the curve of the hips, as does the horizontal line of the square-cut décolleté.

Corset collection
Mainbocher
1939

Suit with corset waist
Lachasse
1948

Black-and-white day dress
Sorelle Fontana
1953

Trompe l'oeil *corset dress*
Antonio Berardi
2009

Asymmetric Dress 2013
Raf Simons for Dior

In Raf Simons's full-length gown, asymmetric beauty results from aesthetic irregularity: the flow of seams on the bodice of the dress—one starting at the center front, the other at the side—spirals in parallel lines around the body, incorporating the shaping darts to provide a form-fitting bustier. Once past the waist, width is added to the pattern pieces, and the resulting volume inflates the silhouette before being draped across the body and caught up on the hip, creating an uneven hemline.

After taking over the helm at the House of Dior in 2012, arch minimalist Raf Simons combined his precise construction methods and simplicity of style with traditional aspects of the heritage brand. Referencing Dior's totemic Corolle line of 1947 and ideal of women as *femmes-fleurs*, Simons's second collection for Dior transforms silk taffeta into a burgeoning bloom of dazzling color. The designer fuses precise architectural layers with a play on volume and transparency, and juxtaposes the molded strapless bodice with a voluminous upper skirt. This is worn over an ankle-length, tubular skirt suspended from the bodice by a sheer panel of silk tulle.

> *I think it's interesting to bring part of minimalism into the world of Dior, but I also want to make it very sensual and sexual and very free."*
>
> **Raf Simons**

Swathes of vibrant yellow silk taffeta create an asymmetric silhouette.

Asymmetric peplum dress
Robert Piguet
1949

Lys Noir evening dress
Dior
1957

> *I love to take things that are everyday and comforting and make them into the most luxurious things in the world."*
>
> **Marc Jacobs**

Jacobs applies head-to-toe, equal-width, monochrome stripes for a 1960s-inspired two-piece skirt suit.

Striped Suit 2013
Marc Jacobs

Stripes are the simplest and most effective of all patterns: they provide a rhythmic surface that indicates movement. However, historically stripes represented disorder, and even today comic-strip burglars and errant schoolboys customarily wear striped clothes. Taking inspiration from the Edwardian blazer, but redirecting the stripes from vertical to horizontal, Marc Jacobs offers a high-waisted shrunken jacket that stops short of the hips, opposing the volume of the mid-calf pleated skirt. The monochrome stripes are meticulously matched across the bodice and sleeves to create an unbroken line, a device that continues across the pleats of the skirt.

Visually, the eye is programmed to seek out straight lines, making stripes one of the most satisfying and versatile print motifs. The eye gives them visual priority as they rarely occur in nature, and consequently the wearer of striped clothes stands out from the crowd. The two-piece skirt suit references the linear composition of Op art and is matched to an oversize tote bag and 1960s-inspired kitten heels. The jacket is neatly curved at the center-front hem, a shape replicated by the high "V"-shape neckline. The revers are folded back to form obtuse angles with the stripes of the jacket.

Op art jacket
Ossie Clark
1965

Black-and-white striped sequin dress
Etro 2013

Striped shirt and trousers
Michael Kors
2013

Striped blazer
Balmain
2013

EXOTICISM

Robe Sorbet 1911
Poiret

Poiret's orientalist evocations provided an exotic alternative to the "S"-shape corset that was prevalent at the time, by offering greater freedom of movement and introducing rich, embellished textiles. The tunic is quartered in cream and black, and the loosely fitting bodice references the square-sleeved kimono, as the fabric is crossed at the center front and caught with a wide, fringed obilike sash. The flat, stylized flowers appliquéd to the overskirt and sleeves are early indications of the influence of Art Deco.

In the early twentieth century, the designs of Paul Poiret manifested a popular interest in "orientalism" that was fueled in part by Léon Bakst's designs for Les Ballets Russes. Poiret's exotic collections included harem pants, feathered turbans, and the iconic "lampshade" tunic of the Robe Sorbet. He initially designed this tunic for his wife to wear to his themed Thousand and Second Night party in 1911, which was held to promote his new designs. The innovative silhouette is created by the stand-away wired overskirt, trimmed with black fox fur. The columnar underskirt is based on the high-waisted Empire line or Directoire line modeled after ancient Greek dress.

"The colors! . . . Colors as sharp as a knife. And the fabrics—the silks, the satins, the brocades embroidered with seed pearls and braid . . . were of an oriental splendor."

Diana Vreeland
fashion editor

The evening gown features the wired overskirt of Poiret's celebrated lampshade tunic.

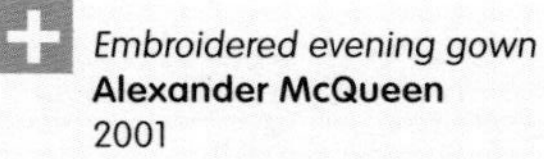

Embroidered evening gown
Alexander McQueen
2001

Chinoiserie collection
Marc Jacobs for Louis Vuitton 2011

Robe de Style 1927

Lanvin

Mysterious, faraway places often fuel a designer's imagination and provide inspiration for form, silhouette, and surface decoration. An avid traveler and collector, Parisian couturière Jeanne Lanvin also studied Eastern and Far Eastern dress. She incorporated the culture of exotic locations into her exploration of design, introducing innovative beading and embroidery techniques into her signature garment, the *robe de style*. This dress combines the tubular bodice and dropped waist that was popular during the 1920s with the panniered skirt and wide-hipped silhouette of the eighteenth century, a period during which the influence of chinoiserie was at its height.

Derived from the French word *chinois* (Chinese), chinoiserie was a style inspired by art and design from China, Japan, and other Asian countries. European designers adopted its motifs and patterns in the eighteenth century, and Lanvin revived it in the twentieth century. This *robe de style* features an appliquéd waterfall of beads, paillettes, and silver metallic thread cascading from the dropped waist to the hem. The ivory silk tulle is gathered over the hips to create a broad skirted effect, and the wide shallow neckline is edged by scalloped embroidery, forming small cap sleeves.

The embroidered chinoiserie motif provides the focal point of the ivory silk evening gown.

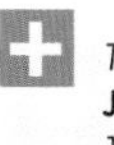

Turkish-inspired tea dress
Jessie Franklin Turner
1919

Robe de style
Vionnet
1939

Careme dress
Christian Lacroix
1987–88

> *"I'm not sure why he [my father] became such a colorist: perhaps it was his Russian blood. Think Fabergé! Mix that with his Florentine roots and you get something explosive and irresistible, yet also elegant and romantic."*
>
> **Laudomia Pucci**

A dramatic photographic shoot on the roof of the Palazzo Pucci captures the diaphanous quality of Pucci's caftans.

Caftan 1969
Pucci

Emilio Pucci fashioned his vibrant polychromatic prints into glamorous versions of the caftan, favored garb of hippies, the protagonists of 1960s counterculture. On the hippie trail to India and Morocco, they sourced vernacular dress, including the simple caftan, a loose-fitting garment open at the neck with deep armholes. These were often cut in one with the body, which was the simplest way of utilizing the width of the fabric. Although caftans were frequently decorated with hand-crafted embellishment at the neck, hem, and sleeves, Pucci merely slashed the fabric to create the neck opening and left open the side seams for the arms. The free-floating panels of the caftan were the perfect canvas for Pucci's intricate, multidirectional allover prints in his favorite color combination of hot pink, orange, yellow, and pale green. Favored by "the beautiful people," such as Elizabeth Taylor and Jackie Kennedy, Pucci elevated the caftan to celebrity status.

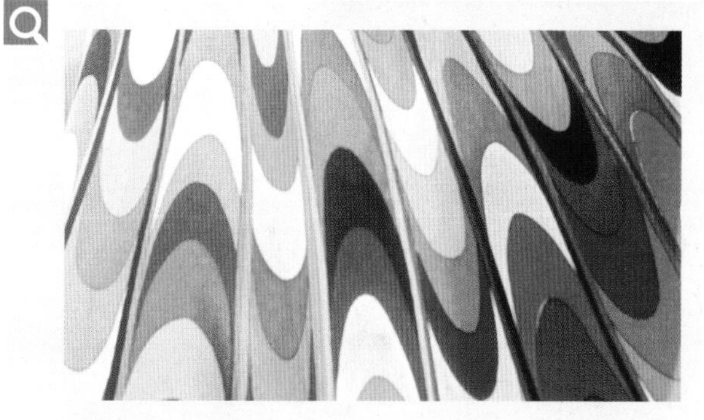

Pucci drew inspiration for his prints from an eclectic array of sources: Renaissance paintings, the regalia of the Palio race in Siena, and the colors and patterns indigenous to various exotic countries. These images were filtered through the medium of his signature style: abstract, nonfigurative form and psychedelic swirls of color, often controlled by borders of contrasting print. These dazzling prints reflected the exotic, color-filled horizons of the new postwar jet-setting clientele.

Robe Sorbet
Poiret
1911

Haute-hippie caftan
Pierre Cardin
1973

Polychromatic slip dress
Christian Lacroix
2004

Toga cocktail dress
Matthew Williamson
2010

Long Evening Ensemble 1976

Yves Saint Laurent

The carmine-colored jacket references an idealized image of the Ukrainian Cossack in its simple edge-to-edge construction and use of braided and beaded embellishment. This is confined to the center front, hem, and cuffs. The matching yoke of the skirt is shaped to the hips from a high waist and edged with a row of black tassels. A simply cut peasant-style blouse in transparent silk chiffon has a tasseled draw thread at the neckline ending in a keyhole opening, secured with a single button.

Elevating folkloric detail to the catwalk, Yves Saint Laurent confirmed the importance of haute couture with his "Russian" collection at a time when prêt-á-porter was in the ascendance. He deployed all the techniques of the seamstresses of the atelier for the collection, which was inspired in part by the costume designs of Léon Bakst for Les Ballets Russes. This richly hued ensemble in the designer's signature duchesse satin fuses a relaxed silhouette with meticulous and lavish attention to detail. The ankle-length skirt falls in stiff folds from the hips, and vertical pockets add insouciance to the formality of the rich, light-reflecting cloth.

"The cut is so ingenious, the fabrics so glamorous . . . that his collections have been the benchmark against which everything else is judged."

Nicholas Coleridge
president of Condé Nast International

The collection was shown in a retrospective at Centre Pompidou, Paris, in 2002.

Costume design for Les Ballets Russes
Léon Bakst 1909–14

Russian Balkan-inspired collection
John Galliano 2009

"I started having a big Kenzo moment too. I loved wearing his pretty, peasanty clothes. Everything Kenzo did was so joyously colorful and naive—a bit like his spectacular fashion shows, which had models dressed as toy soldiers and ballerinas and firework displays."

Grace Coddington
creative director

Kenzo juxtaposes ebullient color and ethnic-inspired printed and knitted pattern in textured layers.

Multipatterned Print and Knit Ensemble 1984

Kenzo

Layering and wrapping the body in loose unstructured garments of varying textures and contrasting vivid color is emblematic of Japanese designer Kenzo Takada's approach to design. Fueled by his preoccupation with the exotic motifs and garment construction that are found in other cultures, he juxtaposes various printed and woven patterns with floral intarsia or jacquard knits. This process was initially prompted by his early days as a student in Paris when he could only afford to buy his fabrics from flea markets. As a result, Kenzo had to mix many bold fabrics together to make one garment, a process sympathetic to the hippie-inspired ethos of the 1970s.

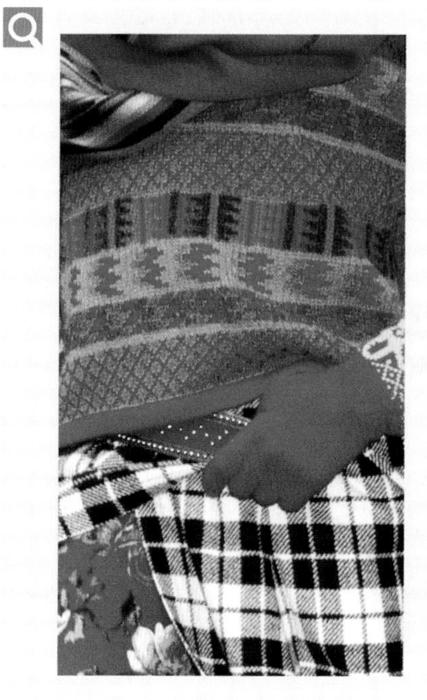

The black-and-white, calf-length pleated plaid kilt is worn open to reveal trousers constructed from a Chinese-inspired, allover floral print on a red background. A matching top is almost obscured by a knitted tank with horizontal bands of color on the body. It comprises a variety of stitches formed with a Fair Isle or punch-card jacquard technique. The drop sleeves feature an intarsia floral pattern of blue on red. Kenzo's eclectic sourcing of pattern includes a Peruvian-inspired print on the shawl draped around the shoulders, the design of the jacquard knit hat, and the matching gauntlets.

Moon and Buddha collection
Bill Gibb and Kaffe Fassett
1975

Tunic and skirt ensemble
Missoni
1975

Multicolored florals
Dries van Noten
2008

Sequin ensemble
Ashish
2010

"It has been Ralph Lauren's cleverness to tap into a submerged global yearning; a yearning for open space and stability and an elusive quality dimly heard of, but never experienced, called Absolute Values."

Nicholas Coleridge
president of Condé Nast International

Lauren pays homage to the contemporary cowgirl with a combination of leather and lace.

Coat Dress and Chaps 2011
Ralph Lauren

Offering an exotic, romanticized perspective of the American Southwest, Ralph Lauren conflates the colors and textures of the landscape with reimagined Western wear and belle époque detailing from the saloon and bordello. A delicately woven plaid coat in palest sky blue and white is cut into a deep swirling curve, longer at the back, that falls from a narrow, form-fitting bodice. The circumference of the coat dress is edged entirely in white cotton Leavers lace (manufactured by British company Cluny Lace), from the high narrow collar to the cuffs of the slightly gathered sleeves. The delicacy of the lace is offset by the tough tan leather accessories and silver hardware.

Adding the hand-crafted accoutrements of the rodeo to the frilled femininity of the coat dress and simple white T-shirt is a broad, tooled, and studded leather belt, fastened with an oversized silver buckle embellished with a bull's head motif. Rather than opting for the clichéd cowboy boot and hat, Lauren has doubled up on the leather, with tan cowgirl chaps—usually worn for protection when riding a horse through bushy terrain—featuring an integrated belt buckled over leather trousers. Unlike trousers, chaps have no seat and are not joined by a seam at the crotch.

Leather lasso dress
Bora Aksu
2008

Macramé dress
Dolce & Gabbana
2010

Navajo jeans and knitwear
Isabel Marant
2011

Suede fringed dress
Moschino
2012

Animal Print Dress 2012

Roberto Cavalli

From a simple, scooped neckline, bound in black silk-satin ribbon, the bodice falls loosely to the waist, where it floats into a series of serried frills. These are deep on the knee-length gathered overskirt, which is also bound in black. Rows of self-fabric narrow frills create volume and are left raw at the edge. Further frills add movement to the hem of the columnar underskirt. Printed with abstract markings in a pale facsimile of fur pelts, the colors stay true to nature: taupe, pale tan, ecru, and black.

Invoking the primal and predatory instincts of wild animals with prints, fur, and skins, Roberto Cavalli invests the female form with a feline presence. The collection was shown on a runway decorated with 40,000 flowers arranged in a tiger-stripe pattern. Here, the mousseline dress is formed from cascades of tiers printed in imitation of layers of fur pelts. In playful juxtaposition, the tailored jacket is the real thing. Skintight, black leather gloves, an accoutrement of the dominatrix, add fetishist overtones. Often associated with the archetypal femme fatale, from the "sex kitten" of the 1950s to the Hollywood screen siren clothed head to toe in leopard print, animal skins are a metaphor for the modern-day huntress.

"Animal motifs and the power that they convey . . . are an extension of all that fascinates me about fashion: the idea of adornment as provocation."

Roberto Cavalli

Roberto Cavalli epitomizes fashion's fascination with reptile and animal skins.

Allover animal print ensemble
Rudi Gernreich
1966

Leopard-skin print all-in-one body
Thierry Mugler 1995

Celebrating the nineteenth-century origins of one of the best-known luxury brands, Marc Jacobs for Louis Vuitton staged a runway show straight from the golden age of steam train travel, rich with the trappings of the belle époque. In acknowledgment of the provenance of the company as luggage maker to European royalty, the model is attended by a porter, in matching livery, carrying three bags. Oversized overnighters or small and formally framed in leather, the bags feature the L.V. logo, in place since 1896 in an attempt to deter counterfeiters. Layers of rich, figured fabrics make up a mid-calf skirt worn over cropped pants, partnered with a classic V-neck cardigan and a dark turtleneck sweater. The elongated silhouette is further exaggerated by the scaled-up, squashed-down velvet hat by Stephen Jones.

Jacobs revisits the accoutrements of aristocratic travel at the turn of the century with a play on proportions and luxurious embellishment.

Belle Epoque Ensemble 2012

Marc Jacobs for Louis Vuitton

For me the reward of doing what we do is doing it, not when it's done. And when people wear it and love it and covet it or can't wait to have it, whatever it is."

Marc Jacobs

The theme of the belle époque is continued in the Art Nouveau patterning seen on the skirt. Characterized by the sinuous lines and curves found in nature, the style originated in the 1880s and was popular until World War I. The skirt features a typical rhythmic design, a free-flowing organic form based on floral abstraction in shades of orange, appliquéd onto a base cloth of black. The flowers are highlighted by the use of holographic shapes in the form of petals. The center front of the skirt is emphasized by a series of large faux buttons, fashioned into the shape of flowers with an outsize crystal at the center.

Ballets Russes-inspired collection
Yves Saint Laurent 1976

Print embellished coat
Christian Lacroix
2007

Embellished black evening coat and trousers
Prada 2012

Astrakan-collared coat for men
Prada
2012

ASCETICISM

I wanted to give a woman comfortable clothes that would flow with her body. A woman is closest to being naked when she is well dressed."

Coco Chanel

In this photograph by Edward Steichen, Chanel's little black dress sets the paradigm for cocktail hour chic.

Little Black Dress 1926
Chanel

An essential item in every woman's wardrobe, the "little black dress" was described by U.S. *Vogue* magazine in October 1926 as "the Chanel 'Ford,' the frock that all the world will wear," thanks to its affordability and the fact that, like the Model T, it came only in black. Previously, black had been worn only at funerals and in mourning, but Parisian couturière Coco Chanel made it the smart choice for the newly popular "cocktail hour," an early evening event that required something less formal than a ball gown. One of the most influential designers of the twentieth century, Chanel produced functional, easy-to-wear clothes that became daily essentials for the modern woman.

Celebrating the freedom of the uncorseted body, Chanel's dress is constructed along the loose-fitting lines and dropped waist of the chemise dress, creating the fashionable garçonne look made popular by the "flappers." The simple crêpe de chine shift beneath the silk chiffon overlay falls just on the knee. A faux bolero is weighted with an Art Deco-inspired border of faceted jet beads. Strands of the beads are also attached to the waistline, creating an overskirt bound around the hips with horizontal rows of decorative stitching before dipping to the mid-calf asymmetrical hemline.

Black sleeveless ankle-length sheath dress
Givenchy 1961

Black lace strapless dress
Balenciaga
1967

Black sleeveless leather dress
Maison Martin Margiela
2002

Black strapless sheath dress
Ralph Lauren
2009

In contrast to the catwalk consumerism of the 1980s, Rei Kawakubo of Commes des Garçons promulgated a nihilistic approach to fashion, overturning accepted notions of "wearability." The designer believed that Western fashion was reliant on a repositioning of historical styles, and sought to break away from conventional form and the effect of historical pastiche and other cultural influences. The lace sweater and padded cotton jersey skirt represent the concept of *wabi-sabi*, a Japanese term used to describe the superior value placed on flawed artifacts through enlightened recognition. The opposite of luxury, the "old and worn" are valued above the "perfect and beautiful," thereby challenging the precepts of good taste. When the collection was first shown in Paris, Western fashion journalists responded with dismay.

Kawakubo explores deconstructionism as an antithesis to Western notions of "fashion."

Lace Sweater 1982
Rei Kawakubo for Comme des Garçons

Fashion is something you attach to yourself, put on, and through that interaction the meaning of it is born. Without the wearing of it, it has no meaning, unlike a piece of art."
Rei Kawakubo

The seemingly random holes in the sweater are the direct result of considered manipulation of the knit process, rather than actual decay. The welted rib of this amorphous sweater is fabricated on a coarse-gauge hand frame using heavy wool. Stocking stitch is perforated in a chaotic process of casting-off and casting-on, and the largest apertures have been elaborated by partial knitting, which produces internal closed selvages. Moreover, the deep two-by-two ribs anchor the garment at the forearms and hip. Kawakubo's use of unrelieved black in the collection inaugurated the noncolor as the signature hue of the fashion avant-garde.

Sweater made from army socks
Maison Martin Margiela
1991

Recycled dress
Xuly Bet
1999

Creation ensemble
John Galliano
2005

Men's deconstructed coat and trousers
Ann Demeulemeester 2012

> *Vulnerability is beautiful to me. There might be a need to fabricate your own beauty paradigms. I guess I never quite bought into any kind of 'standard.'"*
>
> **Hedi Slimane**

Promoting an etiolated silhouette, Hedi Slimane reinvents modern tailoring for the twenty-first century.

Two-piece Slimline Suit 2002

Hedi Slimane for Dior Homme

Hedi Slimane adheres to the inspirational iconography of the slender demigods of music: from the Thin White Duke persona of David Bowie to the 1950s cool of Sammy Davis Jr. and Rat Pack Vegas. The designer's influential skinny silhouette, which initially evolved during his years at Yves Saint Laurent, was carried forward to Dior Homme and ignited widespread enthusiasm for a close-tailored chic and adolescent angularity. Here, the short "bum-freezer" jacket of the late 1950s is styled with a deep-ribboned porkpie hat. Diminutive detailing is used to confound judgments of scale and to reinforce the attenuate line of the figure, emphasized by the narrowly cut trousers resting on the hip. Despite both the sliver of revers and the tiny schoolboy shirt collar barely reaching the threshold of sartorial legibility, there is sufficient resonance in the ribbed tweed of the suit and the regimental stripe of the straight tie to confirm the outfit as a suit.

Slimane's modernist approach to tailoring sparked a new interest in fashion suits among younger consumers, which arguably led to a greater interest in men's tailored clothing in general. With retro verging on mod styling, the padded, square-chopped shoulder line is combined with a high-cut arm scye and tight sleeve. The jacket is adorned with school badges and a watch chain, serving as a subversive adolescent caprice. The diagonally striped narrow tie is of school or regimental significance.

Columnar three-button suit
Brioni
1955

Collarless suit with columnar silhouette
Pierre Cardin 1959

Fall/winter menswear collection
Helmut Lang
2003

Fall/winter menswear collection
Prada
2011

> *[Bottega Veneta] is for everyone, it's for a global world, and it's about objects which are done to be as ergonomic as possible, and to make people's lives better."*
>
> **Suzy Menkes**
> fashion editor

Sports luxe in a simple sheath dress, with Maier's signature refined and understated elegance.

White Dress 2010
Tomas Maier for Bottega Veneta

Driven by a desire for perfection and simplicity, Tomas Maier, creative director of Italian luxury leather goods house Bottega Veneta, has built the brand on subtle, understated design and technical virtuosity. Exemplifying "stealth wealth" with the tag line "When your own initials are enough," Maier redefines glamour with flawlessly constructed clothes that are bereft of extraneous detail. This includes construction seams, which is made possible by the judicious use of double-faced cloth. Recognizable neither by a logo nor extraneous hardware, but by its distinctive construction technique, the fabled Bottega Veneta bag utilizes a method of handwoven strips of leather called *intrecciato,* which is employed here in the construction of the sandals. Combining the restrained simplicity of the sack dress with the relaxed ease of the T-shirt dress, the garment falls to the knees in an uninterrupted silhouette.

In summer white and stripped of detailing, the dress features the quintessential polo collar, which is deepened to a low "V" and left unstructured, forming a serene and uncluttered line to the neck and shoulders. The shaping of the shoulder line is accrued from the extended shoulder seam. Cut in one with the body of the dress, the sleeves end just above the elbow in a deep hem. The placket is created from a simple twist of fabric that runs unseamed from collar to collar.

High-waisted white dress
Derek Lam
2011

Oversized white shirt dress
Stella McCartney
2013

Plissé organza dress
Stella McCartney
2013

Extended cricket sweater dress
Tommy Hilfiger
2013

Leather Tunic 2011
Phoebe Philo for Céline

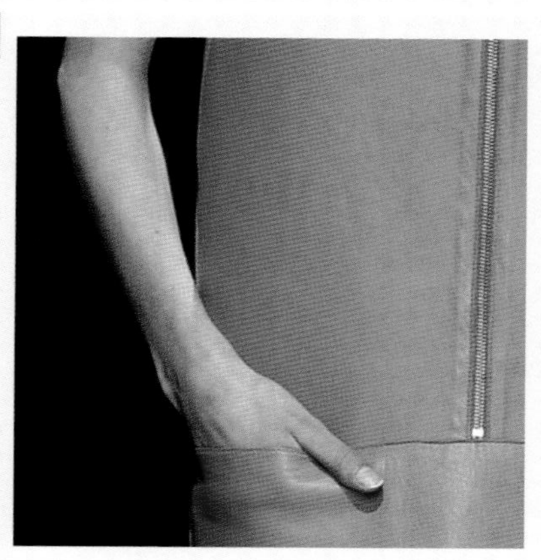

Cut from softest leather in boldest orange, the tunic features deep invisible pockets incorporated into the horizontal seam on the hips. It is bisected by a center-front seam running up to the high round neckline, almost concealing the zipped opening and secured with unobtrusive top-stitching. The refined, unfettered lines of the tunic top are undiminished by any extraneous detail: the armholes and hem are left unbound, and the cut relies on the shoulder and side seams for minimal shaping.

In her 2011 collection for French house Céline, Phoebe Philo exemplifies modern refinement, paring down fashion staples to provide a new, definitive version: shirts are scaled-up and back to front; trousers are loose and long; coats and jackets supersized. Philo rejects formal tailoring for unadorned minimalism and ever simpler shapes, leavening the mix with bright blocks of color within a beige to camel palette, or with unexpected components such as fur-lined sandals. With its origins in military uniform, the tunic—from the Latin *tunica*, meaning layer or membrane—replaces the jacket as a standard partner to pants. The silver metal choker is an independent accessory, not attached to the tunic.

> “*What I love is this idea of a wardrobe. The idea that we're establishing certain signatures and updating them, that a change in color or fabric is enough.*”
>
> **Phoebe Philo**

Razor-sharp leather is cut into an unadorned tunic of color-blocked orange.

Leather halter dress
Ronaldus Shamask
1980s

Tweed cape
Stella McCartney
2013

White Shirt 2012
Yohji Yamamoto

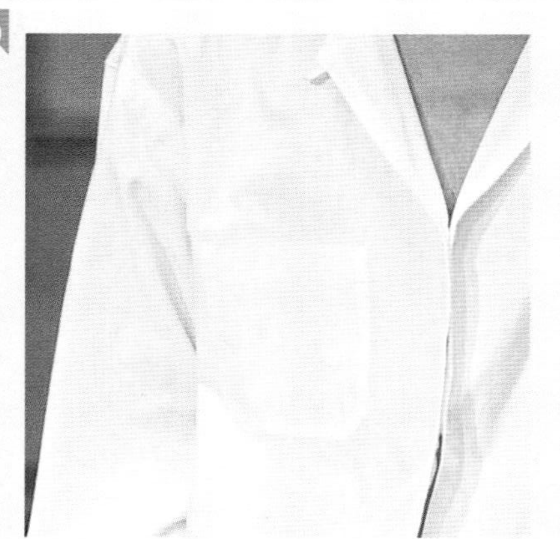

In keeping with the implicit purity of the classic white shirt, Yamamoto applies traditional techniques, including French seaming, to its construction. The narrow revers are left open at chest level, but a small rouleau loop is positioned at the neck to close the center front. The dropped shoulder seam and deep arm scye create a loose, relaxed fit; both of these seams are covered with an off-white textured tape. Two patch pockets are diametrically opposed: one on the chest, the other on the hip.

The ascetic perfection of the white shirt purports to be classless, sexless, and ageless, but like other wardrobe staples it is subject to subtle changes in proportions and finishing details, and can be constructed from various weights and textures of fabric. Although renowned for his avant-garde aesthetic since his emergence in the 1980s, Yohji Yamamoto has always included the white shirt in his menswear collections, exploiting its proportions and fastenings: shrunken or oversized, origami-like folds or buttoned off-center. Here, the oversized shirt is partnered with flowing, butcher's stripe-print "chaps," worn over wide-legged, cuffed pants, revealing a naked ankle.

"If things fit too perfectly, everything looks like a sculpture, not like fashion."

Yohji Yamamoto

Yamamoto's white shirt plays on variations in proportion and volume.

White shirt
Gap
1998

Nilde cotton-poplin shirt
Jil Sander
2013

[The collection] was not about destroying elegance, but achieving a different kind. There was a mixture of the rich and the poor fabrics, a manipulation of fabric and material to mean something else."

Miuccia Prada

Combining couture cut and fabric with dark denim workwear, Miu Miu also references the practicality of the popover dress.

Denim Ensemble 2013
Miu Miu

Referencing a subtle juxtaposition of high and low fashion, Miu Miu combines the workwear origins of dark indigo-dye denim with duchesse satin, the quintessential couture fabric. The satin is used to line the denim shell top, which is shaped to the shoulders with two exterior top-stitched darts exactly aligned to the two slanted patch pockets each side of the center front. These in turn are parallel with the bracelet-length raglan sleeves, which are also top-stitched. With glancing reference to the distressed denim popular with the counterculture in the 1970s, the frayed edges of the pockets are dip-dyed to match the bleached-out patterning on the hem of the tunic.

In the 1940s, during a period of wartime austerity, U.S. sportswear designer Claire McCardell appropriated "humble" fabrics primarily used for workwear, such as gingham and denim, for simply cut functional daywear. The most technically innovative fashion designer of the era, McCardell created the popover dress (left) in 1942, a wraparound dress with a "T"-shape bodice with straight-cut dropped shoulder seams and capacious quilted pockets. McCardell was also the initiator of using double rows of top-stitching, previously found on workman's jeans, as decoration.

Denim jacket
Balenciaga
1995

A-line denim skirt
Stella McCartney
2010

Drop-waist trousers and tunic top
Céline
2011

Denim cape
Maison Martin Margiela
2013

Abstaining from the customary preoccupations inherent in fashion design—polychromatic prints, diverting details, historical revivalism, and ethnic motifs—Jil Sander's pared-down aesthetic represents a paradigm of minimalism in its purity of cut and rigorous austerity of line. Indeed, the silhouette is of overriding importance in the designer's collections, which feature garments constructed using quality materials confined to shades of navy, cream, white, and beige. Returning to her label after a three-year collaboration with Uniqlo, Sander reduces the silhouette to a simple top and oversized gun-metal gray silk culottes, a divided skirt that has been left off the fashion radar for some time. The white top in stiff piqué cotton is split at the center front before meeting again at the neck with a top-stitched tab. The high, indented waist and flared hem are matched to the angles of the cutaway sleeves. Zips spiral around bicolored boots in beige and white.

An exercise in symmetry, Jil Sander signifies luxury with a muted palette and an economy of statement.

Cutaway Top and Culottes 2013
Jil Sander

> *Initially it was the unpractical in fashion that brought me to design my own line. I felt it was much more attractive to cut clothes with respect for the living three-dimensional body rather than to cover the body with decorative ideas."*
>
> **Jil Sander**

With the advent of 1990s minimalism, Sander's understated designs were adopted by the new female workforce, which demanded clothing that reinforced its authority. Sander feminizes the two-piece masculine suit by introducing more pliable materials, lengthening the jacket, and softening the shoulder line. A horizontal seam just below the waist incorporates two flap pockets, their rectangular shape in perfect proportion to the jacket and top-stitched to match the front opening and revers of the jacket. The buttons, and traditionally worked buttonholes, are sited from the waist seam upward to break high on the opening.

Two-piece knitted jersey cardigan suit
Chanel 1916

Double-breasted jacket
Giorgio Armani
1980s

Black leather and organza dress
Helmut Lang
1999

Trouser suit
Margaret Howell
2009

Johnny

SUBVERSION

Lobster Dress 1937
Schiaparelli

Inspired by Salvador Dalí's use of the crustacean in his well-known artwork *Lobster Telephone* (1936), Schiaparelli asked the Surrealist artist to paint a lobster on the center front of her white organza evening gown (left). Thought to denote sexuality and the *vagina dentata* (a folklore motif of a vagina with teeth), the lobster design is positioned directly between the wearer's legs, which is particularly suggestive. The design was interpreted into a fabric print by leading silk designer Sache.

Elsa Schiaparelli subverted the more conventional codes of fashion promulgated by her archrival Coco Chanel, and fused art and fashion by collaborating with avant-garde artists and leading Surrealists of the day, including Salvador Dalí and Jean Cocteau. Following their precepts, Schiaparelli designed a series of garments that displaced the ordinary and placed it within an unexpected and unsettling context. The white silk organza sleeveless evening gown is conventionally cut, with a scooped neckline and an A-line skirt that ends in a deep frill at the hem. The bodice is gathered into a *trompe l'oeil* belt, which takes the form of a stiffened lobster pink inset that provides shaping at the waist.

“*Ninety percent [of women] are afraid of being conspicuous and of what people will say. So they buy a gray suit. They should dare to be different.*”
Elsa Schiaparelli

The influence of art on fashion is seen in this collaboration between Schiaparelli and Dalí.

Cloven-hoof boots
Maison Martin Margiela
2000

Homage to Man Ray
Jean-Charles de Castelbajac 2011

“I had fun making [The Wild One], but never expected it to have the impact it did. I was as surprised as anyone when T-shirts, jeans, and leather jackets suddenly became symbols of rebellion . . .”

Marlon Brando

As gang leader Johnny Strabler, Brando epitomizes the subversive impact of the leather motorcycle jacket.

Black Leather Motorcycle Jacket 1950s
Irving Schott

The motorcycle gangs of the 1950s, epitomized on screen by Marlon Brando in Lászlő Benedek's controversial film *The Wild One* (1953), in which the actor played the leader of the Black Rebels Motorcycle Club, rendered the black leather motorcycle jacket a symbol of rebellion. Brando reputedly wore the Perfecto Model 618, which was first introduced in 1928. The lancer fronted jacket was designed by Irving Schott and named after his favorite cigar, the Perfecto. It was similar in design to the 613 One Star, so called because it had a star on each epaulette. The stars on Brando's jacket were added later by the costume department and placed in the middle of the epaulette rather than in the correct position (for the original 613). As with many totemic items of menswear, such as the trench coat and the T-shirt, the leather motorcycle jacket had military connotations and had been adopted by the Army Air Corps prior to World War II.

Brando provided a template for rebellious, brooding intensity with his uniform of confrontation: jeans, tilted cap, and black leather motorcycle jacket cut close to the body and cropped to the waist. The jacket was constructed from Steerhide, a full-grain leather with a rain- and wear-resistant finish. It features a belted front fastened with a Miter belt buckle (rectangular in shape with mitered corners), D-pocket, flap change pocket, zippered sleeve cuffs, and shoulder epaulettes.

Leather and wool donkey jacket
1929

Melton wool naval peacoat
Schott
1944

Lumberjack check wool shirt
1950s

Western-style denim jacket
1950s

Worn by avant-garde poets, artists, and novelists, the fine-gauge black turtleneck sweater conferred outsider status on the wearer. This aesthetic crossed the Atlantic from New York's Greenwich Village to emerge in the jazz clubs and cafes of the bohemian Left Bank in Paris, and it was also the initial inspiration for Mary Quant's Chelsea Look in London. The nonconformist and anti-establishment status of the turtleneck sweater was appropriated by disaffected youth from the beat generation, epitomized by James Dean both on and off screen. Although often frowned upon in the workplace, the sweater eventually came to provide a sartorially acceptable alternative to the shirt and tie. Worn with close-fitting, drop-waist trousers by Ports 1961, alongside a two-piece suit by Riccardo Tisci for Givenchy, the black turtleneck offers a streamlined silhouette.

Providing androgynous cool, the black turtleneck sweater is used to accessorize contemporary tailoring.

Black Turtleneck Sweater

1950s

The [turtleneck] style horrifies restaurant head waiters, who are still weathering the onslaught of women in pants suits.”

Time magazine

In *Funny Face* (1957), directed by Stanley Donen, Audrey Hepburn stars as a New York beatnik book store assistant who is persuaded to become the muse of a Richard Avedon-style photographer, played by Fred Astaire. She consolidates her intellectual credentials in the film by wearing a black turtleneck sweater paired with narrow black Capri trousers, thereby influencing a generation of women who were eager to emulate her casual style of dressing during a period that was characterized by grown-up decorum. The figure-hugging, fully fashioned sweater, with a small rib at waist, hips, and neck, became a fashion classic.

Sloppy Joe
oversized sweater
1940s

Plain white T-shirt
worn by Marlon Brando
1950s

Back-buttoned
cardigan
1950s

Striped matelot top
worn by Jean Seberg
1960

“I participated in the transformation of my era. I did it with clothes, which is surely less important than music, architecture, painting . . . but whatever it’s worth, I did it.”

Yves Saint Laurent

A 1930s pastiche, and in imitation of Marlene Dietrich, the suit heralds the future wave of feminism.

Pinstripe Suit 1967
Yves Saint Laurent

Although Coco Chanel subverted the wearing of trousers by introducing beach pajamas during the 1920s, these wide-legged trousers in soft, fluid fabrics were suitable only for informal occasions or as leisurewear. Famously worn by the sexually ambiguous film star Marlene Dietrich in the 1930s, traditionally tailored trouser suits were unequivocally associated with deviancy. It was not until the introduction of Yves Saint Laurent's first tuxedo in 1966 that the trouser suit became a fashion staple, and for the first time trousers for women were considered socially acceptable. However, their use continued to be restricted in the workplace and at certain social venues.

This suit is cut along masculine lines, from pinstripe cloth that is more usually associated with the male conservative business suit. However, it is feminized by the waist darts on the jacket and the form-fitting waistcoat worn beneath, which hint at the female form. In contrast, the white shirt and silk foulard tie emphasize the masculine tailoring of the squared-off shoulder line, created with the use of sleeve head wadding. The boot-cut trousers have a deep rise and are cut in the same way as classic men's trousers, with a fly front, turn-ups (cuffs), and a single pleat into the waistband.

Marlene Dietrich suit
Anderson & Sheppard
1930s

Minimalist trouser suit
Jil Sander
1990

Tailored tuxedo
Jean Paul Gaultier
2001

Trouser suit
3.1 Phillip Lim
2009

> *"It's unfashion. Grunge is about not making a statement, which is why it's crazy for it to become a fashion statement . . . Buying grunge from Seventh Avenue is ludicrous."*
>
> **James Truman**
> editorial director

Reflecting the nihilism and rawness of grunge music, grunge fashion exemplified the style of anarchic youth, dubbed "Generation X" by journalists.

Grunge Ensemble 1993

Marc Jacobs for Perry Ellis

The grunge look hit mainstream fashion when New York-born designer Marc Jacobs produced his groundbreaking collection for U.S. sportswear company Perry Ellis. The faux-checked cargo pants are sand-washed silk, printed in imitation of flannel in shades of red and black. These are worn beneath a loosely fitting smock dress in silk, printed with an allover design of large-scale pears. Industrial strength boots from British footwear brand Dr. Martens feature signature yellow stitching and AirWair trademarked soles. Although the beanies, outsize cardigans, and cargo pants were enormously influential, the collection was a commercial disaster.

With its origins in the indigenous clothing of the logging and fishing industries in Seattle—checked flannel shirts and sturdy boots—adopted by local indie-grunge musicians such as Pearl Jam and Nirvana, grunge fashion was initially sourced from thrift stores and vintage outlets. Jacobs eschews the humble materials of Seattle grunge for luxurious fabrics in noble fibers, such as silk and cashmere, for this vintage-inspired, button-through tea dress with a deep frilled hem in printed silk layered over a fine black T-shirt, dressed down with ankle socks and a choker.

Hippie caftan
Hung on You
1967

Seditionaries collection
Vivienne Westwood
1976

Acid house smiley logo T-shirt
1988

Striped knitted dress and coat
Anna Sui
1992

Highland Rape Collection 1995
Alexander McQueen

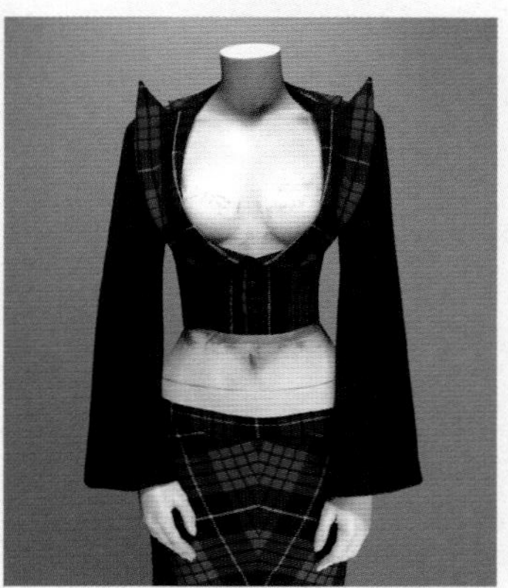

Oscillating between beauty and horror, McQueen's customary trope of implied savagery is combined with glamour, seen here in the match of tailoring and bare breasts marked with wounds from the fray. Referencing nineteenth-century tailoring, the stiffened midriff section of the bodice supplies a corsetlike support, aided by a short row of closely set buttons. The McQueen tartan checks are aligned meticulously on the collar and the razor-sharp, extended revers. The trumpet-shaped sleeves are in green wool felt and extend just beyond the wrist.

Recalling the inhumanity of the eighteenth-century Jacobite Risings and the genocidal nature of the nineteenth-century Highland Clearances, Alexander McQueen attracted criticism for styling his "Highland Rape" collection with distraught and brutalized, blood-stained models. The disarray is evident in the slashed asymmetry of the transparent silk chiffon skirt, featuring imprinted images of heather and bracken. The jacket, pulled back to display bare breasts beneath the roughly constructed silk chiffon top, is tailored from the black, red, and yellow McQueen tartan: a visual signifier of clanship throughout Scottish history and a reference to the designer's Scottish roots.

"People were so unintelligent they thought this was about women being raped—yet "Highland Rape" was about England's rape of Scotland."

Alexander McQueen

Using historic tailoring with surgical precision, McQueen recalls Scotland's violent history.

Pea dress
Maison Martin Margiela
1997

Medea dress
Hussein Chalayan
2002

Since its origins, punk has had an incendiary influence on fashion. Although punk's democracy stands in opposition to fashion's autocracy, designers continue to appropriate punk's aesthetic vocabulary to capture its youthful rebelliousness and aggressive forcefulness."

Andrew Bolton
curator

The dress is invested with the disruptive energy of the seditious upheaval of punk.

Hand-crafted Dress 2008
Rodarte

Adopting the visually confrontational style of the punk movement, Kate and Laura Mulleavy subvert the sweater dress for their label Rodarte by combining anarchic deconstruction techniques with knitted structures. Instigated by Vivienne Westwood and Malcolm McLaren, punk first appeared in London in the mid-1970s, and followers customized traditional garments such as T-shirts, knitwear, and tailoring by ripping, piercing, and printing with subversive images and slogans. Adhering to an aesthetic that encouraged self-customization, punks constructed their own string vestlike sweaters, knitted on very large needles to create large and irregular holes.

The loose singlet dress with its louche mohair volume is anchored only at the neck and arm scye. Rodarte effected the punk ethos of haphazard construction, hand-crafting a fragmented melée of disparate yarns, kabuki colors, and informal stitch structures. The displacement of loose, uneven stitches creates a chaotic surface with irregular patches of black, red, and white in an inventive combination of hand-knit intarsia on a laddered plain-stitch base. Tank Girl combat mitts and studded head-banger bracelets reinforce the playful, styled aggression of the look.

Hangman sweater
Vivienne Westwood
1977

Conceptual Chic dress
Zandra Rhodes
1977

Lacy red and black crop top
BodyMap
1980s

Black lace-paneled dress
Mark Fast
2009

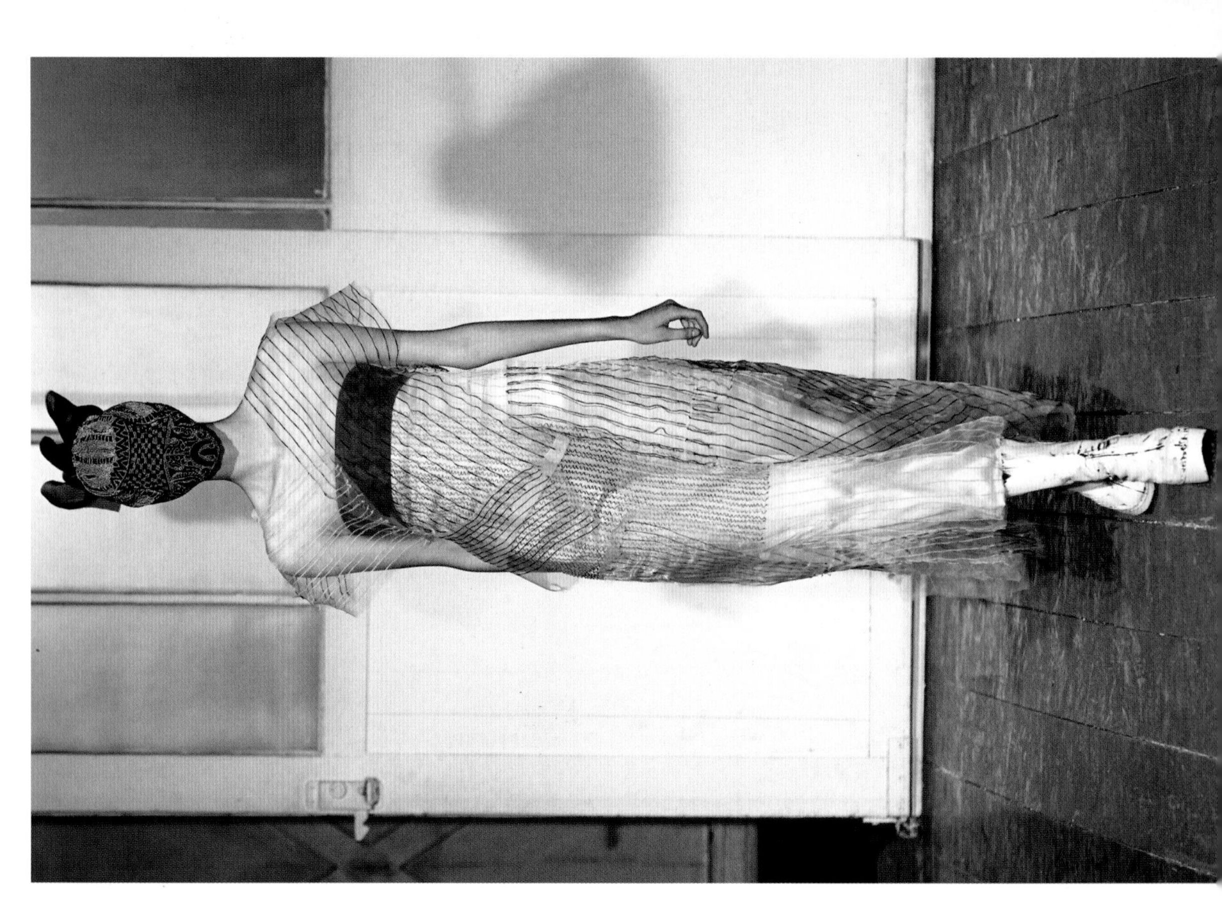

Organza Dress 2013

Maison Martin Margiela

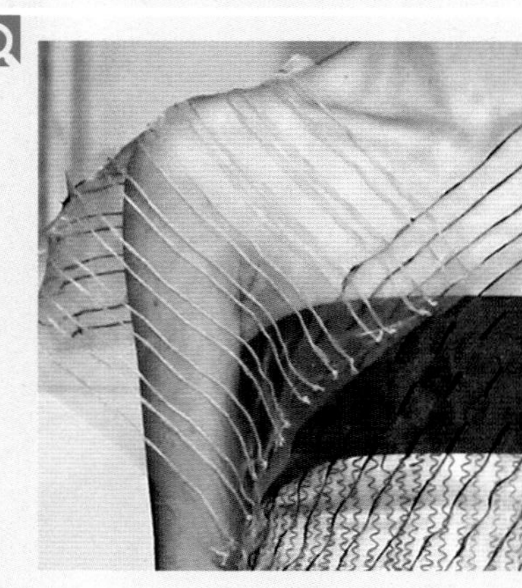

The deconstructed nylon crystal organza, frayed and reflective, is patterned with recollections of the tailor's workroom. The track lines of running stitch recall the satin ticking in the lining of tailored sleeves, or in single formation hint at chalk-striped suiting. Serpentine zigzag baste stitching scribbles an animated pattern of looping yarn, and a multistranded float stitch reads as a passing shadow over a lower layer of transparency. The dark bandeau becomes opaquely variegated by the superimposition of fragmentary layers.

In 2009, twenty-one years after launching his label, the elusive Martin Margiela left his team to progress his vision into the future. The Maison fabricates its garments, by hand, from the residual sediments of previous cultural existences: a recycled garment or leftover fabric. The methods belong to the couture atelier, and many elements are self-referencing to the processes of embellishment and construction. This garment has been assembled directly on the dress stand, using embroidery methods and tailoring stitches to construct nylon veiling in diagonal panels held in place by an underlying broad elastic bandeau. A beaded head square maintains the model's anonymity.

"Often referred to as iconoclast, avant-garde, and experimental, the Maison expresses its creativity through recycling, transformation, and reinterpretation."

Maison Martin Margiela

Averse to superficial styling, the Maison pursues an agenda of deconstructive fragmentation.

Dismembered garments
Robert Cary-Williams
1999

Lace and organza dress
Preen
2013

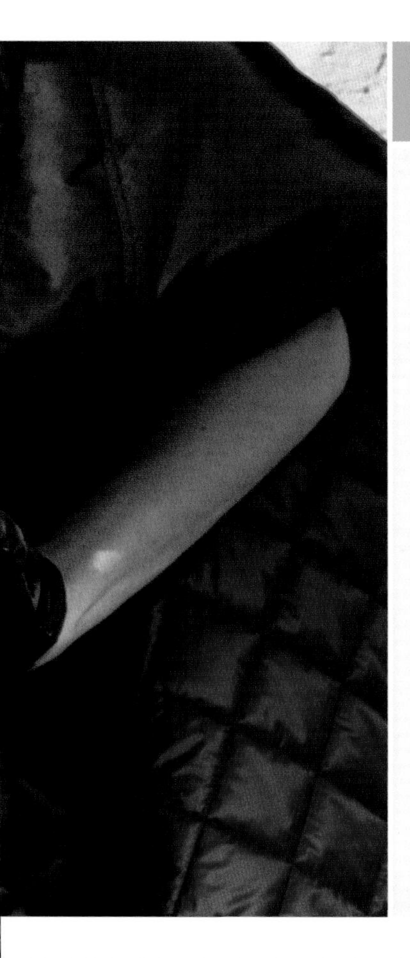

UTILITY

"Burberry has its own DNA. I describe it as disheveled elegance, this beautiful craftsmanship with something a bit broken up. That's very close to my personal view on design. That's probably what is different."

Christopher Bailey
Burberry chief executive

The Burberry trench coat continued to retain its military-inspired features during the 1930s and beyond.

Trench Coat 1914
Burberry

A quintessentially English brand, Burberry was founded in 1856 by Thomas Burberry, but the company legacy began in 1880 with the invention of gabardine, a utilitarian, hard-wearing yet breathable fabric made from yarn that was waterproofed before weaving. These qualities made it an ideal material for the practical raincoat that followed. Only made in beige, the Burberry coat is double-breasted not only for extra warmth but also to provide another layer of waterproof fabric on the main part of the body, and the whole is pulled in with an adjustable self-fabric belt. The epaulettes are designed to hold a folded hat in place, and the buckled straps on the sleeves to prevent water running up the arm. The revers of the high-standing collar can be fastened up to the neck, with further protection provided by a "storm flap" buttoned across the center front. Roomy vertical pockets on each hip obviate the need for a bag.

In 1914, Burberry was commissioned by the British War Office to adapt the heavy, rubberized weatherproof coats worn by officers to suit the conditions of trench warfare, and the result was the lightweight "trench" coat. The iconic coat was adopted by the armed services as part of the uniform, including in the United States by the Women's Radio Corps, seen here in c. 1919. The belted waist, mid-calf hemline, and full skirt of the coat reflect the emerging barrel-shaped fashionable silhouette.

Flying jacket
Amelia Earhart
1928

Perfecto motorcycle jacket
Schott NYC
1928

All-in-one siren suit
Roger Piguet
1939–40

Utility suit
Victor Stiebel
1942

Beach Pajamas

1920s

A new category of practical clothing known as resort wear emerged alongside mass tourism during the 1920s and 1930s, when sunbathing and swimming became popular pastimes. Offering freedom of movement, beach pajamas soon became a seaside staple, and the wide-legged trousers were also worn off the beach for sporting activities such as golf (left). They were made in easy-to-wear fabrics, such as stretch jersey, linen, or *éponge* (toweling), and incorporated dressmaking details such as decorative buttons, bows, and self-fabric belts. Printed fabrics often featured the chevron stripes and sunray motifs of the Art Deco style.

Popularized by Coco Chanel's appropriation of sailor's trousers in the 1920s, beach pajamas were first worn over swimsuits, before being partnered with a separate top and jacket. As with evening wear, fashion's focus was on the bare back, and beach pajamas were characterized by a deep, "U"-shape, back décolletage, a complex arrangement of straps, or a halter neck. Triangular inserts known as godets provided extra volume around the hem, and elasticated shirring gave shape around the waist and hips.

> *I gave women a sense of freedom. I gave them back their bodies: bodies that were drenched in sweat, due to fashion's finery, lace, corsets, underclothes, padding."*
>
> **Coco Chanel**

Enjoying the freedom of jersey wide-legged trousers, a group of women head for the beach.

Three-piece silk pajamas
Jean Patou
1929

Sportswear pajamas
Clare Potter
1937

Palazzo jumpsuit
Anne Klein
1964

Beloved of style icons such as Grace Kelly and actress Anne Crawford (left), the twinset has sustained its popularity since its appearance in the 1920s and 1930s. Originally categorized as sportswear by the manufacturers, the British twinset was not initially "designed" but engineered by the framework knitter. The introduction of the designer into the process occurred in the 1930s, when the Pringle company partnered a long, loose, high-button cardigan—made for export to the United States and later known as a "sloppy Joe"—with a simple, round-neck, short-sleeved sweater. Knitted in a fine and light yarn, worn together they resulted in the classic twinset. Minor adjustments to the neckline and sleeve length followed, but the basic premise remains the same: the two garments are invariably constructed in the same color, yarn, and stitch.

The fully fashioned twinset in pastel cashmere has proved a wardrobe staple.

Twinset 1930s
Pringle

Our aim is to ensure that everyone who wears a Pringle sweater experiences a feeling of luxury and comfort, and hope that an increasing number of well-dressed women all over the world will appreciate . . . 'It's not only the name . . . that tells you it's a Pringle.'"

Pringle of Scotland

Representing restrained good taste, and produced in a variety of yarns from summer-weight cotton to luxurious cashmere, the twinset was a must-have garment not only for stars such as Margot Fonteyn (right) but also for the 1950s housewife. Worn with the cardigan slipped casually over the shoulders and partnered with a tweed skirt, the twinset provided a paradigm of practical, flattering daywear. The shaped sweater features a deep ribbed hem, and the innate elasticity of the yarn yields to the contours of the body, defining the hourglass figure that was prevalent at the time. The only decorative detail is the row of outsize buttons.

Square-neck tank top and raglan cardigan
Bonnie Cashin 1955

Oversized twinset
Giorgio di Sant'Angelo
1972

Ankle-length twinset in apricot cashmere
Halston 1975

Merino wool twinset
John Smedley
2012

"I have often said that I wish I had invented blue jeans: the most spectacular, the most practical, the most relaxed and nonchalant. They have expression, modesty, sex appeal, simplicity."

Yves Saint Laurent

Immortalized on screen in Lee 101 jeans and white T-shirt, James Dean wears the rebel uniform of a generation.

Blue Jeans 1950s
Lee

Functional and durable, with a provenance in the sixteenth- and seventeenth-century, indigo-dyed cotton from Nîmes, France (denim), and sailors trousers from Genoa, Italy (jeans), blue jeans were adopted as workwear in the nineteenth century by an itinerant workforce. The following century, mediated through the image of film stars such as James Dean in *Rebel Without a Cause* (1955), denim jeans evolved from being the utility workwear of the American West to representing disaffected youth. Of the three cornerstone brands—Levi's, Lee, and Wrangler—it was Lee that capitalized on Dean's mythically wayward persona, astutely aligning the star with its jeans.

Established by Henry David Lee in Kansas in 1889, the Lee company initially manufactured workwear. Its original denim jeans borrowed from Levi's and included its chief rival's double-arcuate, back-pocket, signature stitching and rivets, but these were replaced with bar tacking and the "lazy S" back-pocket stitching for Lee 101 Riders, first produced in 1946. The same year, Lee introduced the "twitch" back label, which resembled the hot branding of a steer's hide. Adding to the effect of deliberate sartorial indifference, the indigo-cast denim is worn faded and distressed by Dean.

Storm Rider 101J denim jacket
Lee
1932

11MWZ jeans
Wrangler
1946

Twisted to fit jeans
Levi's
2001

Distressed denim collection
Ralph Lauren
2010

Leotard 1985
Donna Karan

A reinvention of the leotard, the halter-neck "body" in stretch jersey features poppers between the legs to prevent it from riding up and to provide a smooth contour beneath the waist. Worn here with a wide belt to accentuate the waistline, the garment forms the basis of a collection of interchangeable pieces, primarily in black, of supple stretch wool jersey and cashmere. Sensuous yet practical, and with the emphasis on the quality of the materials, the pieces are devoid of any extraneous decoration.

With her easy-to-wear, interchangeable capsule collection "Seven Easy Pieces," Donna Karan offered a system of dressing that fulfilled the desires of the aspirational, urban woman for no-fuss flattering workwear. It was an alternative to the hard-edged tailoring and big-shouldered corporate dressing of the era, and featured garments that were designed to take women from office to evening with a minimum of effort, eliminating the need for choice at the start of a busy day. The garments were designed to cover every basic clothing need, and included pull-on pants, a sarong-style skirt, man-tailored jacket, sweater, scarves worn wrapped around the shoulders or hips, and a simple cashmere dress.

I don't believe there has been a designer who has more consistently and thoughtfully addressed the complex needs of the modern dresser."

Anna Wintour
editor-in-chief

Karan's first own-label collection is synonymous with the New York look.

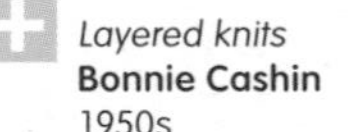

Layered knits
Bonnie Cashin
1950s

Urban tweeds and sweaters
Ralph Lauren
2001

“*Now the Adidas I possess*
for one man is rare
Myself homeboy got 50 pair
Got blue and black cause
I like to chill
And yellow and green when
it's time to get ill
Got a pair that I wear when
I'm playin' ball
With the heel inside make
me 10 feet tall.”

Run-DMC
"My Adidas"

The trademark look of hip-hop group Run-DMC conflates 1980s "bling" with sportswear by Adidas.

A-15 Tracksuit 1987
Adidas

Dominating the old-school hip-hop aesthetic, Adidas was the brand that was most closely linked to Run-DMC, not least because of the $1.6 million endorsement deal that began in 1986, the same year that Run-DMC released the hit "My Adidas" at the peak of their popularity. Rap was not then the cultural behemoth it would become, and the foresight to associate with the hip-hop movement meant that Adidas was the dominant youth sports brand for most of the 1980s, although other sports brands were adopted and revered in particular cities, with Reebok being popular in Philadelphia, for example. By spring 1987, the fruits of the Run-DMC/Adidas collaboration were released and included a range of sneakers, sweatshirts, T-shirts, and the leather tracksuits shown here, which were known by their serial number A-15. Each bomber jacket-style tracksuit top had the easily recognizable three Adidas stripes and the trefoil logo.

Run-DMC released their album *Tougher than Leather* in 1987: the same year that these leather tracksuits were made. Although the garments appear to be purpose-made for sport, the idea of athleticism is subverted by the use of leather, which is impractical for heavy exercise. The trefoil logo was introduced in 1971 to reflect the brand's expansion into clothing. After much development, the design of three leaves intersected by the triple stripe was chosen to signify the diversity of the Adidas brand.

D-1 leather flight jacket
worn by U.S. air force
c. 1941

Adidas tracksuit
worn by Noel Gallagher
1994

Versace for H&M
worn by Kanye West
2011

Adidas collection
worn at Olympic Games Opening Ceremony 2012

"I wanted something longer and looser, something sensual and feminine, but utilitarian at the same time."

Joseph Altuzarra

A hybridized, quilted, poncho-style parka offers both practicality and high fashion.

Parka 2011
Altuzarra

Given a Manhattan edge by U.S. luxury ready-to-wear brand Altuzarra, the parka has its origins in the heavy, hooded jacket lined in caribou fur that was introduced by indigenous groups of the Arctic region to combat freezing temperatures and ferocious wind speeds. The garment evolved into the distinctive fishtail parka worn by the U.S. army serving in the Korean War in 1951; this version featured an attached wolf-fur hood, heavy cotton outer layer, and detachable lining, as well as a "fishtail" designed to be tied around the legs for extra insulation. The parka was adopted as a signifier of cool, urban youth by "mods," a postwar British subculture, who sourced the garment from army and navy surplus stores. Here, Altuzarra straightens the back hem, leaving it capelike and square, the blouson front cut short to the thigh. Insulation is provided by the seamed lightweight outer layer and the red silk quilted lining.

The deep-set raglan sleeves of the parka are roomy enough to fit over tailored outerwear. The quilted seams lead to the high, stand-up, wraparound collar, which is lined in fur and fastened with Velcro. Worn down, the attached hood features knotted and metal-tipped drawstrings pulled through metal-framed eyelets. Pragmatism is evident in the zipped vertical breast pockets set on either side of the shaped quilted seams. The close-fitting red windbreaker is by L. L. Bean.

Vexed parka
Vexed Generation
1995

Parka/poncho
Alexander Wang
2011

Satin-twill parka
Burberry Brit
2013

Delancey parka coat
Marc by Marc Jacobs
2013

Jumpsuit 2012
Stella McCartney

The patterned fabric is cut away above and below one arm, revealing the shoulder to the neck. The cutout is replaced with an Aertex-inspired, see-through, power-mesh sports fabric down the side of the body. Replicating the Rococo volutes found in the anatomy of stringed instruments and their convolute curves—saddle and scroll, neck and tailpiece—the edges of the fabric are isolated from the areas of foulard block-repeat print by a padded three-dimensional whorl of heavy white Italian cording embroidered in satin-stitch.

After appearing on the runway for several seasons, the jumpsuit—more generally perceived as a utilitarian one-piece garment used to insulate and protect the body for a range of activities—now enjoys classic fashion status. For 2012, Stella McCartney keeps the loose, easy-fit lines of the original garment—with a slightly dropped crotch and wide, ankle-length pants—but cuts away one side of the jumpsuit in a high-fashion statement. The fluid patterned viscose features a foulard-type print with a diagonal stylized floral pattern in navy blue and gold on white. A simple round neckline and a single set-in sleeve provide contrast.

“I love that you can have the language between the two worlds of technology and fashion, because I don’t think that many designers get to do that.”
Stella McCartney

Stella McCartney reinvents the jumpsuit as a modern fashion classic for 2012.

Floral jumpsuit
3.1 Phillip Lim
2013

Shorts all-in-one
Rag & Bone
2013

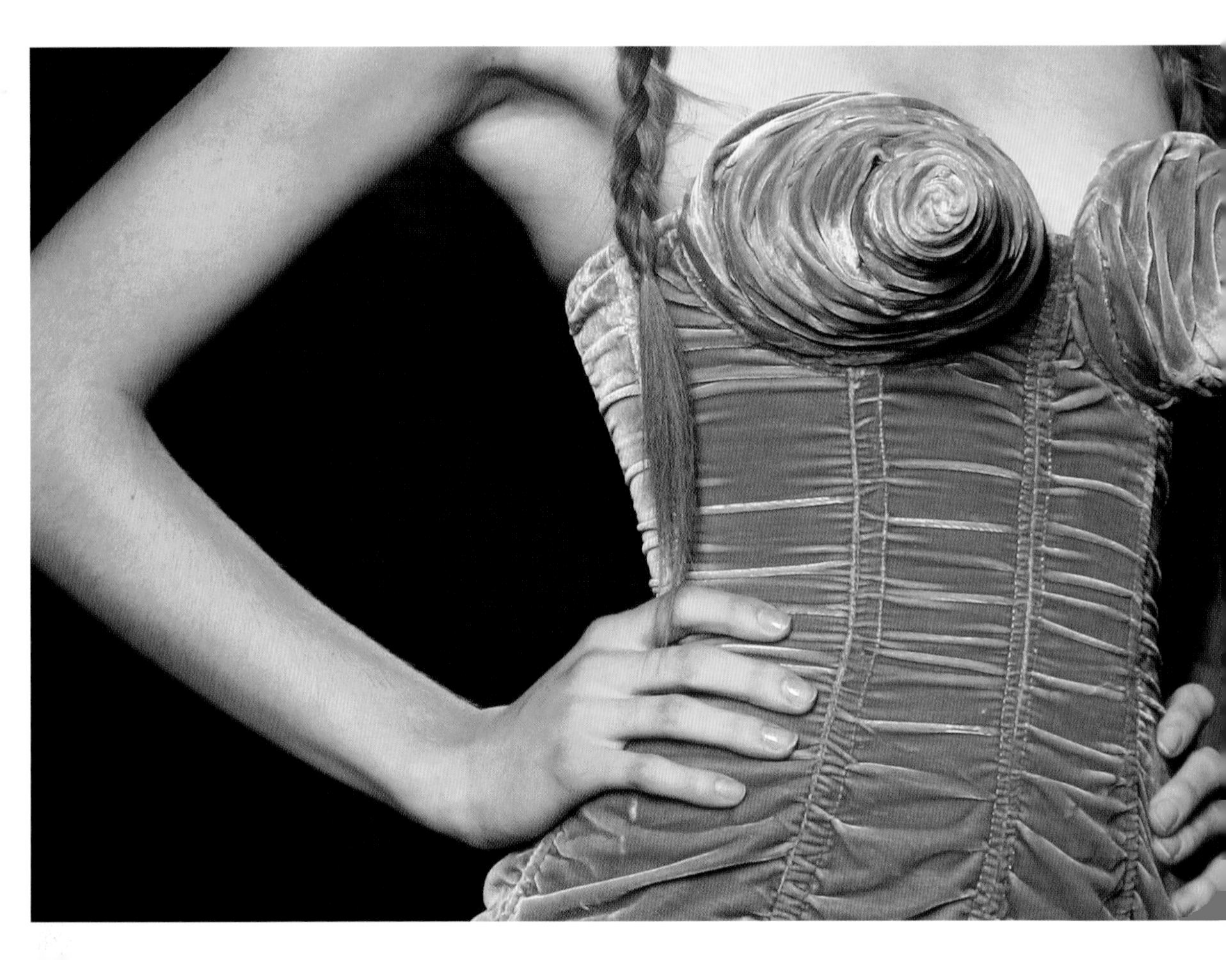

EROTICISM

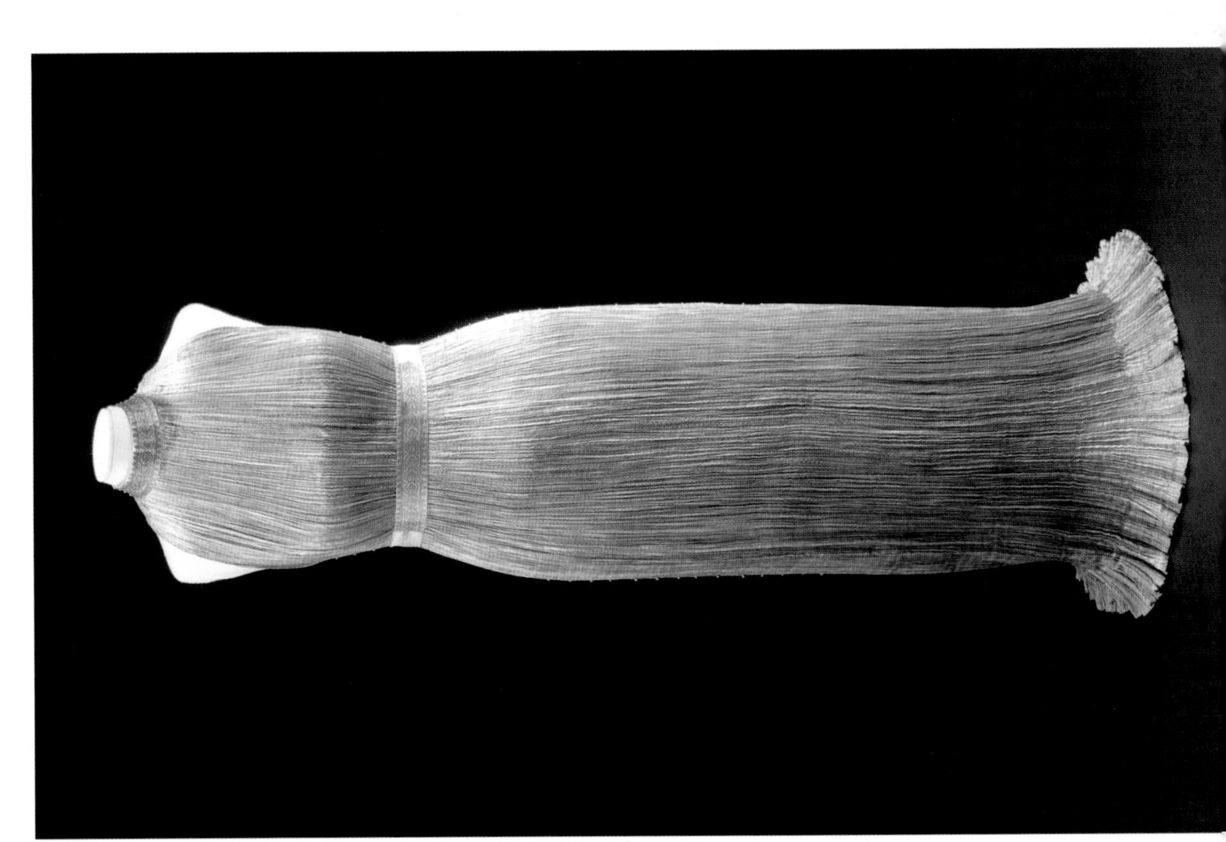

Delphos Pleated Dress *c.* 1920

Fortuny

Sensuality is a covert form of eroticism, one that is subtle in approach and reliant on the senses. The shimmering ripples of pleated silk over the undulating lines of the body, the nuanced distinction of the breasts, and the silver color of the tussah silk—the tones of which change according to the light and movement—all exemplify sensuality. Although originally designed to be worn as a tea gown for informal occasions at home, the Delphos dress began to be worn as evening attire by the avant-garde of the era, including the creator of modern dance, Isadora Duncan, and her daughters (left).

Attracted by the classical dress of ancient Greece and the eroticism inherent in the uncorseted body, Mariano Fortuny created the Delphos series of dresses between 1907 and 1949. The gowns were constructed from pleated silk, using a unique process that remains undisclosed. It is probable that the cloth was stitched by hand with a basting thread that was pulled in tightly at the end of the panel. Redolent of the fluted dress of antique statuary, the line of the gown extends to the ground, where it is weighted, thus creating a columnar silhouette.

Of all the indoor and outdoor gowns that Mme. de Guermantes wore, those which seemed most to respond to a definite intention, to be endowed with a special significance, were the garments made by Fortuny y Madrazo."

Marcel Proust
novelist

The liquid softness of the dress is derived from Fortuny's use of tussah silk.

Neoclassical gown
Tom Ford for Gucci
2003

Pleated silk dress
Yohji Yamamoto
2005

Bikini

1952

After her appearance in the aptly titled film *The Girl in the Bikini* (1952; left), the erotic appeal of French film star Brigitte Bardot became forever associated with the bikini. In Roger Vadim's drama *And God Created Woman* (1956), she consolidated her role as archetypal sex kitten. French couturier Jacques Heim and Swiss engineer Louis Réard invented the near-nude two-piece swimsuit in 1946, and it symbolized an era of postwar freedom and sexual license. Revealing several erogenous zones—back, upper thigh, and navel—the bikini caused social and religious outrage, and it was not until the 1960s and a new era of sexual permissiveness that the bikini was widely accepted.

Pin-up girl and screen goddess Marilyn Monroe wore the forerunner of Bardot's bikini in 1951: a two-piece swimsuit comprising a structured halter top and substantial bottom half that covered the hips from waist to thigh, revealing only the rib cage. It was constructed along the lines of outerwear, with a draped deep knicker concealed with an apronlike wrapped skirt, edged in a frill and fastened with a button on the waistband. The top replicates the circular stitching seen on 1950s bras, but connotations of underwear are lessened by the frilled edges of the all-concealing cups.

The stretch fabric top comprises two unsupported triangles, and the briefs are cut low on the hips.

Emerald green bikini
worn by Jayne Mansfield
1955

Belted white bikini
worn by Ursula Andress
1962

Fur bikini
worn by Raquel Welch
1966

> *Haute couture is like an orchestra, whose conductor is Balenciaga. We other couturiers are the musicians and we follow the directions he gives.”*
>
> **Christian Dior**

Theatrical impact and luxurious craftsmanship epitomize Balenciaga’s approach to couture.

Evening Dress 1953
Balenciaga

Aspiring to romanticism rather than classicism, celebrated model Suzy Parker and photographer Norman Parkinson epitomized the era's cult of femininity, expressed through a fastidious formality combined with a louche glamour. The luxurious déshabillé of the ball gown by Cristóbal Balenciaga and the seductive image of the half-robed cherub on the painted theatrical backdrop are offset by the groomed perfection of the maquillage and the small black hat secured on the crown of the head with a white camellia, the ostrich plume wittily extended to provide playful movement. Balenciaga's masterly cutting technique combines a dropped shoulder seam with a narrow sleeve that allows freedom of movement. The deep, wide, "V"-shape neckline falls loosely from the shoulders, leaving them bare and providing a setting for the parure, a matching set of white metal and pearl costume jewelry.

Unlike the prevailing hourglass figure of the 1950s, this silhouette is simple and understated, following the line of the body without any extraneous padding or armored infrastructure. The natural waistline is marked by a seam, and the fitting darts are lost in the texture of the figured silk brocade in softest pink. Juxtaposing the expanse of the décolletage is the formality of the opera gloves, narrowly fitting and over the elbow, and the length of silk taffeta twisted around the shoulders and arms.

Poppy-patterned evening dress
Balmain
1956

Flowers of the Fields of France evening dress
Norman Hartnell 1957

Floral-patterned silk ball gown
Erdem
2008

Ice-blue frilled goddess gown
Rodarte
2008

Conical Bra Dress 1984

Jean Paul Gaultier

Promulgating the concept of underwear as outerwear, Gaultier transformed the corset from its conventional purpose of restraint into an erotic device of empowerment. His totemic designs for Madonna's Blond Ambition world tour in 1990 (left) subverted traditional ideas of seduction and femininity by projecting the female body into a public space—less to do with sexual arousal and more to do with aggressive self-presentation. In this costume, the cone-shaped cups of the bra stitched in concentric circles and the restrictive waist push the female silhouette to its extreme.

The wearing of lingerie-inspired clothing is an erotic device that is traditionally utilized by women to enhance their femininity, and it is often concerned with titillation or seduction. In the conical bra dress by Jean Paul Gaultier, the boudoir influence is referenced in the use of rayon velvet, ruched around the torso in imitation of the bones and stays of a traditional corset. However, garments associated with the boudoir can provide a different thrill, one of waywardness and subversion. Gaultier creates breasts that follow an upward and outward trajectory, prohibiting entry into the wearer's space.

"I have loved corsets since I was small. When I was a child, my grandmother took me to an exhibition and they had a corset on display. I love the flesh color, the salmon pink satin, and the lace."

Jean Paul Gaultier

Eroticism is subverted with Gaultier's signature use of the corset in ruched rayon velvet.

African collection
Yves Saint Laurent
1967

Bra dress
Moschino
1988

Fashion is everything. Art, music, furniture design, graphic design, hair, makeup, architecture, the way cars look—all those things go together to make a moment in time, and that's what excites me."

Tom Ford

Ford combines classical simplicity with an homage to U.S. 1970s minimalism and the drapery of Halston.

Cutout Dress 1996
Tom Ford for Gucci

Tom Ford's second outing for Gucci as creative director of the brand consolidated his reputation as the leading exponent of hard-edged 1990s minimalism combined with an erotic allure. In this gown from his collection of white columnar dresses, the narrow binding of the deep scooped neckline is extended to hold together the center front of the bodice, thus creating a circular cutout that plunges to below the naval and draws attention to the gilt hardware and its implications of space-age purity. The gilt buckle is suspended independently and held in place over the naval by a narrow tie looped around the edge of the buckle, the ends hidden beneath the dress.

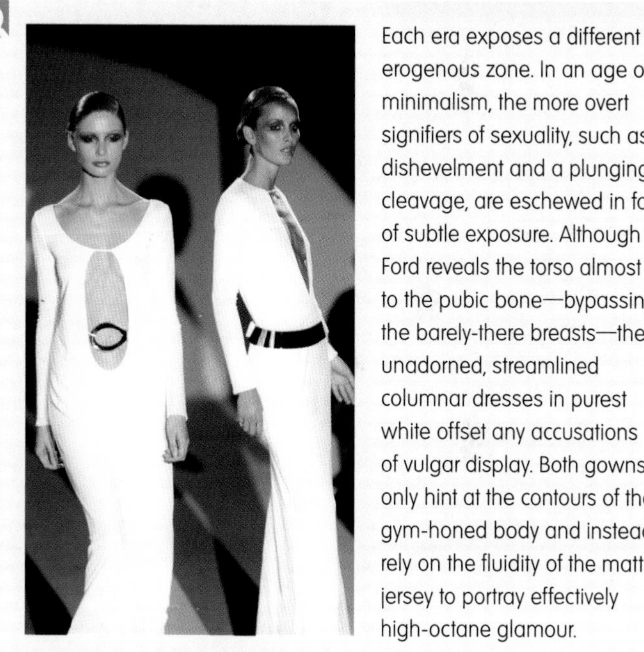

Each era exposes a different erogenous zone. In an age of minimalism, the more overt signifiers of sexuality, such as dishevelment and a plunging cleavage, are eschewed in favor of subtle exposure. Although Ford reveals the torso almost to the pubic bone—bypassing the barely-there breasts—the unadorned, streamlined columnar dresses in purest white offset any accusations of vulgar display. Both gowns only hint at the contours of the gym-honed body and instead rely on the fluidity of the matt jersey to portray effectively high-octane glamour.

Cutout evening gown
Jean Patou
1934

Evening gown
Balmain
1961

Matt jersey halter dress
Geoffrey Beene
1975

Halter dress
Halston
1980

Corset 1996
Alexander McQueen

Alexander McQueen combines the erotic allure of black lace with a seamed and boned corsetlike carapace to achieve a fierce gothic romanticism. Unlike the ironic and playful "underwear as outerwear" aesthetic promulgated by designers such as Vivienne Westwood and Jean Paul Gaultier, McQueen's deployment of the corset is one of serious intent, a powerful expression of unequivocal sexuality with connotations of fetishistic and sadomasochistic practices. Traditional elements of the boudoir, such as black lace highlighted with faceted jet beads, are rendered darkly erotic by the tailoring of the extreme pointed revers.

The corset is the means by which the female body is subjected to forcible restraint; it is a device to tighten and control the parameters of the silhouette. In McQueen's corset, the tension inherent in the molded form is emphasized by the extended stiffened revers that rear up and pierce the air on either side of the face. The lace is appliquéd to the bodice, which is cut to reveal the stitching beneath, and positioned to emphasize the smallness of the waist, curving into a deep "V"-shape point. The line runs parallel to the lace on the hips, which is scalloped into a "U"-shape curve.

McQueen counteracts the sculptural form of the corset with fragile embellished lace.

Bondage collection
Versace
1992

Ribbed corset crinoline dress
Gareth Pugh
2008

Olivier Theyskens collection
Nina Ricci
2009

“Fashion always has to be about changing and moving forward, to make people dream. My job now is to make our aesthetic evolve while remaining truly Versace—I want to make dresses that every woman wants: sexy and jaw-dropping—I always want it to be relevant but I also want it to be always about glamour.”

Gianni Versace

Held in place with a single jeweled clasp, the dress was one of the most photographed gowns of 2000.

Bamboo Print Dress 2000
Versace

The transparent silk chiffon of this boldly erotic gown has a vivid jungle print of foliage and bamboo in shades of green. The dress was designed to flaunt as much flesh as possible with only the minimum coverage required for public decency. Acknowledged as Donatella Versace's breakthrough dress after she took over the label on her brother's death in 1997, the gown was first seen on the catwalk worn by Amber Valletta but later became the favored style of assorted celebrities, including Jennifer Lopez who wore it to much acclaim to the 42nd Grammy Awards. The gown is currently exhibited in the Fashion Museum in Bath, England, as dress of the year for 2000.

More than a mere red-carpet ensemble, this showgirl gown was worn by celebrities to generate maximum publicity, and to attract the attention of a paparazzo eager for a glimpse of naked flesh. It is apparently held in place with only a citrine-studded jeweled clasp at groin level, creating the focal point of the dress, and the slightest movement reveals the full-length of the legs to the hips. The precariousness of the plunging bodice is secured with invisible double-sided adhesive lingerie tape. Modesty is further preserved by a pair of knickers in a matching bamboo print.

Strapless evening gown
Sorelle Fontana
1954

Safety-pin dress
Versace
1994

Diamond-encrusted dress
Julien Macdonald
2001

Net and embroidered dress
Elie Saab
2002

Lace Dress 2013
Elie Saab

The silver and white lace motifs float on the surface of nude-colored net, the transparency of the fabric belying the demure high neckline of the gown. It gives the illusion of nakedness, offering tantalizing glimpses of skin beneath the lace, yet conceals with denser patterning where necessary. Named after the city of Chantilly, France, the lace is known for its fine ground pattern outlined in cordonnet, a flat untwisted strand; the design was made for Saab by French lace manufacturers Sophie Hallette.

Described as "an ode to delicateness" by couturier Elie Saab, this full-length lace evening gown features a fluid, tulip-shaped skirt. The corded pattern scrolls down the arm and body, its contours lavishly embellished with iridescent beadwork yet remaining light as air. With its origins in the cutwork and bobbin lace of the sixteenth century, lace was a laboriously hand-crafted textile used only for collars and cuffs until the invention of machine-made lace in the nineteenth century. Historically associated with cascading wedding veils and trains and the seductive underpinnings of the boudoir, such as the peignoir, or negligee, lace is now a winning formula on the red carpet.

> *If a woman doesn't want 'rich,' she doesn't come to couture."*
>
> **Elie Saab**

The subtle allure of encrusted lace both reveals and conceals the body.

Nude lace gown
Giambattista Valli
2012

Nude chiffon and lace appliqué gown
Alberta Ferretti 2013

REVIVALISM

It was a flea market, but on Saturdays it changed. Lord Kitchener's sold racks of tunics; there were boas, those old fox stoles, second-hand fur coats, pith helmets, Victorian dresses, bits of Victorian furniture, general junk."

Robert Orbach
I Was Lord Kitchener's Valet

Pete Townshend wears a Union Jack jacket accompanied by members of English rock band The Who, formed in 1964.

Union Jack Jacket 1966
I was Lord Kitchener's Valet

The demand for the new and the novel in fashion is often followed by a period of retrenchment and a plundering of historical styles. In the mid-1960s, space-age minimalism was replaced by a revival of interest in Victoriana, including ceremonial military tunics and flags. The London retail emporium I was Lord Kitchener's Valet, named for the British Field Marshall and former Commander-in-Chief of the army in India, revived the military uniforms of colonial Britain and purveyed them as a symbol of "Swinging London." This jacket is constructed to take advantage of the strong graphic lines and coloration of the Union Flag, popularly known as the Union Jack.

Irony in fashion presents an image that is contrary to its meaning. Traditionally a symbol of patriotism, the Union Jack is deployed here as a decorative device, thus undermining the postimperial values of the past. It consists of a red cross, a red saltire, and a white saltire on a blue ground. The red cross of St. George, patron saint of England, edged in white, forms the center of the jacket, broadest at the waist and extending into the narrow revers. The red is superimposed on the white saltire of St. Andrew, patron saint of Scotland, and blue forms the ground color of the jacket.

Harris Tweed collection
Vivienne Westwood
1987–88

Union Jack jacket
Alexander McQueen
1996

Pirate collection
John Galliano
2001

Union Jack jacket
Russell Sage
2008

"What made Ossie very, very special indeed, and unlike anyone else around, was his sense of proportion. That's what changes fashion."

Prudence Glynn
fashion writer

The fluid lines of the dress are emphasized by the engineered print.

Handkerchief Point Dress 1969

Celia Birtwell and Ossie Clark for Quorum

The free-thinking and minimalist 1960s segued into the 1970s under the influence of a revival of the patterns, motifs, and fabrics popularized by the Art Deco movement. The denial of the modern in favor of the nostalgic was one way in which to express individuality in fashion, and this, in turn, led to the revival of a more complex and fluid silhouette, exemplified by the intricately cut clothes of Ossie Clark. The long, lean lines of the handkerchief point dress, shaped with two parallel seams running though the bust point, flare out into godets. These triangular inserts are delineated with bands of geometric pattern that disperse throughout the body of the garment.

A design movement that dominated the decorative arts for two decades, Art Deco originated in Paris, and the style was first exhibited in the city in 1925 at the Exposition Internationale des Arts Décoratifs et Industriels Modernes. Popular Art Deco designs, such as stepped stripes and sunray motifs, can be seen in this allover engineered print designed by Celia Birtwell, with the emphasis on the handkerchief points of the hem. The silk chiffon dress, a perfect synthesis between garment and pattern, is photographed worn by French model Amanda Lear (left).

Cape and dress
Jean Patou
1931

Peacock feather print dress
Matthew Williamson
2004

Paisley print dress
Etro
2006

Chrysler Building print dress
Holly Fulton
2011

"Some may claim John Galliano as the original fashion fantasist but Bill Gibb did it first. His emotional feeling for opulent fabric, rich texture, and rainbow colors dominated the fashion world in the decade after the decline of the mini."

Lynn Cochrane
journalist

Referencing the Renaissance, Bill Gibb incorporates geometric patterning with florals.

Multipatterned Dress and Jacket 1970
Bill Gibb for Baccarat

Of the many themes that constitute revivals in fashion, Bill Gibb incorporated both the historical and the rural in this multipatterned dress inspired by the cut and structure of Renaissance clothing and the pastoral prettiness of floral prints. The jacket is cropped to a high waist and stiffened to form a scooped neckline of stepped curves edged in braid, held together with a ribbon rosette. The narrow sleeves of the jacket are slashed in the Elizabethan manner and joined once at the elbow, marked with long ribbon streamers, allowing the billowing sleeves of the dress to be pulled through. The checkered pattern that forms a deep border at the hem is replicated at the waist, where the fabric is looped over to form a double peplum, thereby creating an interruption in the long, voluminous, pleated skirt. This emanates from a high waistband caught under the bosom in line with the edge of the jacket.

The juxtaposition of pattern in scale, subject matter, intensity, and materials is an essential element of dress that is perceived to be bohemian. Worn by hippies and the avant-garde during the late 1960s and early 1970s, bohemian dress rejected the man-made in favor of accoutrements purloined from peasant costume, Romany dress, and elements of historical clothing. Bill Gibb finessed this eclectic aesthetic to produce high-end fashion of immaculate workmanship.

Indian feather sunspray dress
Zandra Rhodes
1970

Tie-dyed silk poncho and trousers
Halston 1970

Chiffon and velvet evening dress
Thea Porter
1971

Chamois and floral print dress
Giorgio di Sant'Angelo
1973

> *People ask, 'How can a Jewish kid from the Bronx do preppy clothes?' 'Does it have to do with class or money?' It has to do with dreams."*
>
> **Ralph Lauren**

An insouciant pose by Redford as Gatsby shows off traditional tailoring with a 1920s twist.

The Great Gatsby Suit 1974

Ralph Lauren

Ralph Lauren's depiction of Jazz Age elegance for Jack Clayton's adaptation of *The Great Gatsby* (1974) paved the way for a new interest in fashion nostalgia during an era of stylistic confusion. Although Theoni V. Aldredge received an Academy Award for her costume designs for the film, it was Ralph Lauren's styling of the male actors, and Robert Redford as Jay Gatsby in particular, that introduced the label to a wider audience. The three-piece suit with straight-edged, double-breasted waistcoat (vest) in brown with a chalk-white pinstripe is worn with a white deep-collared shirt and double-knot Windsor tie. The breast pocket of the jacket features the requisite three-point handkerchief. Lauren took inspiration from the yearbooks of Princeton, Harvard, and Yale, and from old photographs of prominent Americans, to promulgate the aesthetic of a classic U.S. heritage, on which he built his fashion empire.

The film associated the Ralph Lauren label with upper-class U.S. style and the "preppies," who were privileged students of the pre-college preparatory East Coast schools who shared certain characteristics of dress. The preppy look had always featured in mainstream U.S. style, but in the 1970s it became recognized internationally as high fashion. The off-duty uniform included cashmere sweaters, button-down shirts, and cuffed chinos (below).

Neo-Edwardian suit
Savile Row
1950

Three-piece suit
Tommy Nutter
1972

White tuxedo
Antony Price
1973

Three-piece suit
Brooks Brothers for Leonardo DiCaprio as Gatsby 2013

I want to get back to the position where couture becomes a kind of laboratory for ideas, the way it was with [Elsa] Schiaparelli. The new couture should be all about theater. One dress for one woman for one character; you dress the actress or the part she has to play."

Christian Lacroix

Lacroix designed this silhouette-changing pouf skirt for the House of Patou.

Pouf Skirt 1987

Christian Lacroix for Patou

In his final collection for the House of Patou, Christian Lacroix introduced historical revivalism to a decade that was renowned for sharp-shouldered power dressing. The designer revolutionized the prevailing silhouette by referencing the eighteenth century with his adoption of the corseted figure and voluminous skirt. He combined elements of the vernacular clothes of his native southwest France and Spain with opulent fabrics and artisanal effects that recalled a more luxurious and leisured age. The form-fitting black velvet jacket is decorated in the style of the *traje de luces* (suit of lights) and is embroidered in gold, as befits a *matador de toros* (bullfighter). Accessorized with neat button boots, the model balances a *sombrero cordobés* with veiling on her head. In 1988, the groundbreaking collection was awarded the Dé d'or, a prize given by the international fashion press to the best couture collection of the year.

Aligned to the style of the eighteenth century, an era frequently referenced by Lacroix, the increasing volume around the hem of the skirt widens out from the narrow waist, which is obscured by the small peplum of the fitted jacket. The circumference of the silk duchesse satin skirt is gathered in below the knees and pulled under, thereby creating the signature "pouf" silhouette. The burnt orange of the balloon-shape skirt is overlaid with a multidirectional print in dark brown.

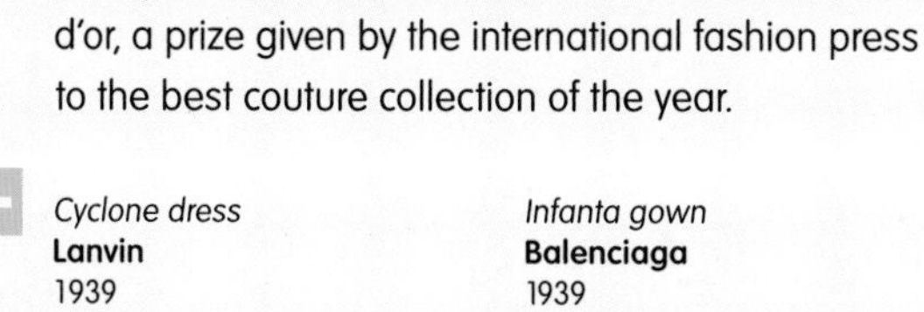

Cyclone dress
Lanvin
1939

Infanta gown
Balenciaga
1939

Crinoline evening gown
Jacques Fath
1951

Evening ensemble
Karl Lagerfeld for Chanel
1990

Maria-Luisa Ball Gown 1998

John Galliano for Dior

The ball gown is not only a highly visible symbol of wealth and status, but also presents a romantic view of women in the sway of the voluminous skirt, the neatness of the corseted waist, and the allure of the rounded bosom. All these elements reference an idealized version of femininity rooted in the New Look introduced by Christian Dior in 1947. Like the *robe á la française* (left), the bodice of Galliano's gown features a "stomacher," a stiffened triangular section of fabric inserted into the front that ends in a rounded point just below the waist, keeping the carriage upright. This pre-revolutionary style historically included front lacing, decorated with ribbon bows of decreasing sizes called echelles.

John Galliano's eclectic sourcing of historical detail includes an appropriation of definitive styles from two centuries. In the Maria-Luisa dress, he revives the bodice of the eighteenth-century *robe á la française* and combines it with the crinolined skirt of the mid-nineteenth century, when its circumference was at its widest. The use of black was confined to mourning protocol until the twentieth century; here it adds to the drama of the silhouette and is unrelieved except for roundels of appliquéd goffered frills.

> *With the acuity of a dress historian and the vision of a creative maestro, Galliano, in one dress, outlines the history of French fashion, as well as the history of the House of Dior."*
>
> **Andrew Bolton**
> fashion curator

Romantic grandeur in black silk recalls the formal court gowns of previous eras.

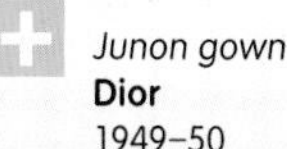

Junon gown
Dior
1949–50

Crinoline evening gown
Jacques Fath
1951

Black-and-white evening gown
Christian Lacroix
1987

Planet Gaia 2010
Vivienne Westwood

In 2010, Westwood refreshed the insolent punk evangelism of her own genesis to inspire the new generation to care about the planet. She drew on the power of Mother Earth mythology to continue her career as fashion's demagogue, working messages such as "Act fast, slow down, stop climate change" into the collection. A calf-length duster coat in crystal organza—symbolizing the ozone-threatened troposphere—encloses a "Loyalty to Gaia" front-laced and peplumed corset from her pagan era, tied with a ribbon at the waist.

In her "Planet Gaia" collection, Vivienne Westwood references an ideal version of the past at the same time as posing questions about culture, art, and society. Within a single outfit, she readily combines an eloquent diversity of fabrics with typical raw, distressed edges and imagery. The graffiti-print, ankle-grazing trousers are adorned with a monochrome rustic engraving of a pre-industrial Eden of flora and fauna. They are cut low on the hips to display the boxer shorts beneath, which are patterned with the serpentine print motif seen in the "Pirate" collection (1981).

"We have the choice to become more cultivated and therefore more human—or by muddling along as usual we shall remain the destructive and self-destroying animal, the victim of our own cleverness."

Vivienne Westwood

The "Loyalty to Gaia" print corset is a symbol of self-discipline and restraint.

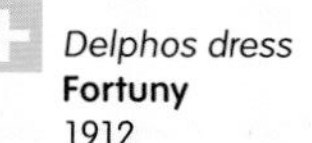

Delphos dress
Fortuny
1912

Goddess dress
Rodarte
2008

“I hate decorative details that have no purpose. I love buckles, for example, but I hate it when I see a jacket covered with buckles that have snaps behind them and it’s all fake.”

Tomas Maier

Tomas Maier employs 1940s-style soft tailoring to provide a fashion classic of vintage-inspired femininity.

Tea Dress 2013
Tomas Maier for Bottega Veneta

The tea dress entered the fashion lexicon as a wardrobe staple at the turn of the twentieth century, and continues to be shown in one form or another every spring/summer season, usually featuring a floral print. In his collection for 2013, Tomas Maier gives the garment retro styling and a 1940s vintage feel, with the emphasis on a strong shoulder line created from a slightly gathered sleeve head and fluid, narrow skirt. This impression is enhanced by a double row of pleating, pressed outward from the center front, and the austere touch of self-fabric covered buttons. The natural waist is defined by a narrow belt secured with stylized patterned butterflies.

In the 1870s, women adopted déshabillé, a semi-fitted or loose gown, as a relief from corsets. Initially worn exclusively indoors, often while indulging in the rising middle-class habit of taking afternoon tea, this more relaxed style of dress evolved into daywear for informal occasions. Commonly made from exotic fabrics and combining elements of historical dress, the tea gown was popularized by U.S. designer Jessie Franklin Turner in the early twentieth century (left). Designed in the 1920s, this gown features a bird pattern discovered by Turner on a black-and-white tunic from Bukhara, Uzbekistan.

Peapod print dress
Givenchy
1953

Floral-print cotton dress
Laura Ashley
1970s

Seed-packet print dress
Erdem
2010

Printed chiffon tea dress
Ralph Lauren
2012

THEATRICAL

Tailored Suit 1930s
Adrian

As head of costume at Metro-Goldwyn-Mayer film studios during the 1930s and 1940s, Adrian worked with many of the renowned female stars of the day. However, it was with Joan Crawford that he had his most enduring connection, responsible for dressing the star for twenty-eight of her films, including *Mildred Pierce* (1945; left). Deciding to emphasize rather than disguise the actress's broad shoulders, Adrian introduced the shoulder pad, thereby setting the trend for the wide-shouldered and narrow-skirted silhouette that would prevail throughout the decade.

The sharpness of Adrian's tailoring is emphasized by the use of striped cloth, created by textile designer Pola Stout. The suit is masterfully designed and constructed, with a low break at the center front of the jacket leading to the extended revers, which further widen the appearance of the shoulders. The cinched-in waist is caught with a single button. Glamour included impeccable grooming: the suede gloves match the handheld clutch, and the feminized trilby adds to the businesslike appeal of the suit. A brooch, the era's favorite accessory, is pinned here at the neckline of the softly tailored silk blouse.

> *I never go outside unless I look like Joan Crawford the movie star. If you want to see the girl next door, go next door."*
>
> **Joan Crawford**

Adrian's tailored suit features his signature manipulation of striped cloth.

Utility skirt suit
Hardy Amies
1946

Tailored trouser suit
Yves Saint Laurent
1967

Renowned for the theatricality of his aesthetic and conflated narratives, John Galliano combines 1940s Hollywood glamour with the art of burlesque. This lengthy, teasing dance, in which the performer almost disrobes, was perfected by iconic movie stars such as Marlene Dietrich and Lauren Bacall. Here, the gown is styled up to replicate the pose of screen siren Rita Hayworth, including the tumbling red locks and over-the-elbow gloves. Galliano fixes the focal point of the gown at the waist, from where the spangled tulle scrolls upward over the nude satin base to the shoulder. Similar embellishment featuring faux jewels travels diagonally across the body and downward to encircle the hips, creating a stiffened, jeweled part-peplum on either side. Ombréd silk chiffon—from purple to palest blush pink—forms a small train at the back of the dress.

State-of-the-art glamour in sheer silk chiffon, overlaid with bejeweled belle époque-inspired embellishment.

Strapless Gown 2005
John Galliano for Dior

"The idea of cultures colliding is something that continues to inform the way I work, research, and create."
John Galliano

Rita Hayworth, star of the silver screen, fused full-on glamour with the provocative nature of burlesque in her luminous appearance in the noir melodrama *Gilda* (1946; right), directed by Charles Vidor. One of the best-known dresses in film history, the black satin strapless gown, split to the thigh and tied on the hip with an oversized bow, was designed by Columbia Studios costumier Jean Louis. In the film's signature moment, Hayworth sashays her way through "Put the Blame on Mame" while seductively peeling off her long gloves and tossing her mane of hair. The bodice is built over a boned foundation to secure it in place.

Lys Noir evening dress
Dior
1957

Scarlet corset dress and opera cape
Dolce & Gabbana 1992

One-shouldered red satin dress
Vera Wang
2011

Duchesse satin bustier gown
Raf Simons for Dior
2013

Gothic Ensemble 2009
Nicole Farhi/Michael Kors

A transparent black silk tulle dress by Josef Statkus half obscures a prim white blouse with an upstanding frilled collar by Nicole Farhi, and ropes of outsize faceted jet beads by Lee Angel are twisted around the model's neck. Calf-length, laced button boots meet a goffered black silk petticoat by Chanel, worn beneath a Michael Kors red coin-spot skirt. Chantilly lace gloves cover the hands to the cuffs of the blouse. The model half lies along a black fur rug covering a leather chaise longue. She represents a louche and dissolute Edwardian elegance, even though there is no area of skin exposed.

The Grand Guignol theater, once based in the Pigalle area of Paris, explored themes of revenge, love, and hate, titillating the audiences with its macabre and twisted world of horror. The plays were at their most popular in the early nineteenth century, and contained scenes of psychological and sexual menace, themes summoned up in this fashion shoot by photographer Craig McDean. The model's languid pose betrays an altered state, her face concealed by the tulle veil and a rope noose clasped limply in her hand.

"Beauty is also submitted to the taste of time, so a beautiful woman from the belle époque is not exactly the perfect beauty of today, so beauty is something that changes with time."
Karl Lagerfeld

Vogue Italia controversially features shocking and provocative images.

Madonna's dress for "Frozen"
Olivier Theyskens
1998

Black leather and goat hair jacket
Julien Macdonald 2011

Black leather corset
Gareth Pugh
2013

Thanks to its long history and experience, fashion has become a worthy ambassador for Spanish creativity, culture, and identity. In addition to Spain's innovation, there is also the quality of Spanish craftsmanship and its long tradition."

Spanish Ministry of Education, Culture, and Sport

Subtle references are made to the Pierrot ruff and pantaloons of the circus clown and commedia dell'arte characters.

Pierrot Ensemble 2009

Amaya Arzuaga

Taking inspiration from the late seventeenth-century Italian traveling troupe of players known as the commedia dell'arte, the origin of the contemporary circus, Spanish designer Amaya Arzuaga references one of the principal characters: the sad clown Pierrot. The deep purple strapless bodice in light-reflecting sequins is molded to the body before flaring out into a stiffened peplum-length skater skirt. The waist is emphasized by a broad, black, silk-satin cummerbund tied at the back in an outsize obilike bow. The substantial ruff of the second skirt is attached above the knees. This has the effect of changing the proportions of the body, creating a disjointed, acrobatic figure by implying two indented waists. Beneath the frilled and stiffened skirts is a pair of loose, pantaloon-type trousers in silk tulle by Armand Basi, caught in at the ankle above wedge-heeled, peep-toe shoes by Moschino.

More customarily worn around the neck of the Pierrot clown to frame the face, the deep frilled ruff of stiffened organza is here displaced to just above the knees to create a short, almost horizontal skirt: the obverse of the rigid and padded upturned frame above. The undulating wired edges of the transparent organza frill, in palest silver gray, are decorated at the front with swathes of ruched black and purple silk-satin ribbon, interspersed with neat matching rosettes.

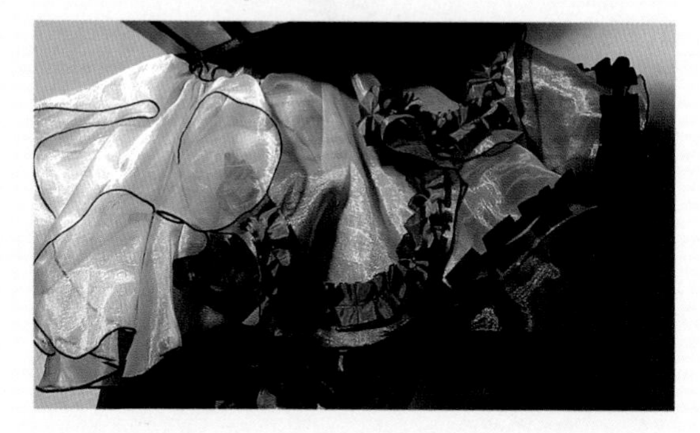

Roundabout skirt
Manish Aror
2009

Lady Gaga dress
Nicola Formichetti
2010

Pierrot collar suit
Walter van Beirendonck
2013

Wired bustier and peplum skirt
Dolce & Gabbana
2013

Art Nouveau Gown 2011
Marchesa

Chapman and Craig channel the marchesa's decadent aesthetic of operatic glamour for a modern audience. The bodice is directed away from the waistline to form butterfly wings of Art Nouveau-inspired black piping on pink, the angle and pattern replicated in the ogee-shaped peplum. This is cropped at the waist to curve gently around the back of the dress, forming a carapace-like structure. The nude silk tulle forms the fragile basis for a columnar skirt that falls from a high waist to a fishtail train.

A legend among her contemporaries, fin de siècle socialite Marchesa Luisa Casati astonished society by parading with a pair of leashed cheetahs. She favored the fashions of designers such as Mariano Fortuny and Paul Poiret, and the latter's innovative "lampshade" tunic from 1912 is replicated here for the red carpet by British designers Georgina Chapman and Keren Craig, who co-founded the Marchesa label. Like Poiret's design, inspired by costume designer Léon Bakst's orientalist creations for Les Ballet Russes, the gown has a dipped overskirt wired to stand out from the wearer and stiffened with mirrored whorls of corded embroidery, also seen around the hem.

[Marchesa Luisa Casati] lived such a fantastic life. She literally saw herself as a living work of art."

Georgina Chapman

Fin de siècle glamour in nude silk overlaid with black, from red carpet favorites Marchesa.

Théâtre des Champs-Élysées gown
Poiret 1913

Fin de siècle bias-cut gown
John Galliano
1997

"I like imagining what it would've been like to go to those clubs in London in the early eighties, like Taboo and Kinky Gerlinky, where everyone dressed up and made themselves into something different every night. It all looked like such fun."

Edward Meadham

Eighteenth century-inspired opulence subverted by scarlet tulle and jewel-encrusted trousers.

Embellished Tulle Dress 2013
Meadham Kirchhoff

In subverting the regal grandeur of the eighteenth-century court of Versailles and the fashions of Louis XVI's mistress, the renowned *grande horizontale* Madame de Pompadour, and his profligate wife Marie Antoinette, Anglo-French design duo Edward Meadham and Ben Kirchhoff deploy a plethora of gathered silk tulle and a multiplicity of crystals. The sweetheart line of the corseted bodice, richly embellished with clusters of rhinestones in royal blue and scarlet, is partially obscured by a close-fitting transparent silk tulle top, also encrusted with a scattering of tiny crystals. Multicolored outsize jewels decorate the neck, hands, and wrists.

Inspired by eighteenth-century Rococo design—an elegant asymmetric style derived from natural forms—and the paintings of François Boucher, the silk tulle mid-calf skirt is padded around the waistline to form slight panniers. This line is emphasized by a series of royal blue, silk-satin bows of differing sizes in the style of echelles. Historically, these were placed in order of size down the center front of an eighteenth-century bodice. The profligate use of scarlet and blue crystals is also seen on the narrow-leg trousers beneath the skirt and on the Roger Vivier-inspired kitten heels.

Eventail cocktail dress
Dior
1956

Silver leather bustier and tulle skirt
Vivienne Westwood 1988

Eighteenth century-inspired dress with religious iconography
Jean Paul Gaultier 2007

Yellow dress with bows
Christian Lacroix
2008

Ombré Dress 2013

Prada

A cluster of stylized chrysanthemums, known as *kiku* in Japan, is overprinted on one shoulder, one hip, and again on the hem, forming a triangle of color on the metallic gray ground of the dress. The flower is associated with notions of rejuvenation and longevity, and was historically the flower that represented the Imperial House of Japan. Digitally printed in ombré color to match the spray-paint effect of the ground, the orange-red blossoms are formed from half-open petals amid a halo of white.

With a base fabric ombréd in white on gray to replicate metal, the dress was inspired by the armor and artifacts worn by the samurai, the military nobility of pre-industrial Japan. A square breastplate is attached to the deep round collar, with stylized red petals appliquéd around a white circular center (the obverse of the Japanese flag.) The high-waisted dress is dissected with pressed-in knife edges and stitched seaming along the bust line and halfway down the cuffed sleeves, appearing as indentations made in metal. *Tabi*, traditional Japanese socks, provide inspiration for the shoes, with separation between the toes.

“*Dream is forbidden, nostalgia is forbidden, and to be too sweet is not good. Everything we used to feel historically, now you can't enjoy. The clothes are the expression of this impossible dream.*”

Miuccia Prada

The stiff satin dress combines elements of samurai armory with floral motifs.

Kimono-style evening jacket
Edward Molyneux
1926

Japanese-inspired collection
Alexander McQueen
2001

> *Fashion is fashionable again. You can see the effect in the number of companies that sell copies. Also, what's interesting is that I can see women on the streets in what was maybe a Balenciaga silhouette. It's pretentious maybe to think that you created that look or influenced her. Maybe she is wearing somebody else but, in the end, on the street, you can see the influence."*
>
> **Nicolas Ghesquière**

Ghesquière's use of monochrome enhances the architectural purity of the line.

Ruffled Skirt 2013

Nicolas Ghesquière for Balenciaga

Between 1937 and 1968, Spanish-born Cristóbal Balenciaga was celebrated for his sculptural and architectural sense of design, many of his garment shapes echoing his strong religious and artistic background. As creative director, Nicolas Ghesquière applies a modern sensibility to the heritage of the couture house, as seen in the severity of the monastic-style top and the deep ruffles of the Spanish-influenced skirt, resonant of Cristóbal's dress design in *c.* 1968. The shoulder seam of the cropped cotton gabardine bodice is extended to form a perfectly flat plane, bypassing the outlines of the body and marked only by a series of flat, angular folds in the cloth.

The expressive *el baile flamenco*, danced at gitano weddings and celebrations in Spain, was the inspiration for Ghesquière's black velvet crêpe skirt, which fits closely to the hips before flaring out into an asymmetric cascade of rigid ruffles, high at the front and dipping deep at the back. The ruffles are formed by circles of fabric opened out and applied to the straight edge of the opening of the skirt, originating high on one hip. The motion of the wearer exposes the white underside of the frills, and the edges of the fabric are left raw to provide further definition to the graphic movement of the skirt.

Dress and jacket of gold ikat silk
Givenchy
1989

Lace and chiffon gown
Julien Macdonald
2011

Laser-cut lace frills
Marchesa
2011

Silk and acetate cantilevered dress
Antonio Berardi 2013

FUTURISM

Casbah Dress 1965

John Bates

Transparency in dress has many meanings, and changing attitudes toward appropriate dress are inevitably related to the culture of the time. When fashion is preoccupied with youthful attributes, it becomes an expression of modernity rather than seduction, as in this see-through minidress modeled by Jean Shrimpton (above). The mesh insert linking the upper and lower elements of the dress provided an acceptable level of exposure at a time when clothes were at their most minimal.

Concealment and exposure are intrinsically linked to ideas about the fashionable body. During the space-age era of the 1960s, designers deployed futuristic materials, such as plastic and metallics, for brief easy-to-wear garments that allowed freedom of movement. John Bates modernized the dress by elevating the waistline and the hem, thus emphasizing the midriff. He appropriated unusual materials and utilized a knitted mesh, more usually used for men's string vests, to hold the bra top and miniskirt together. The print is a geometric design in the style of Moorish tiles.

"There was a universal movement afoot that wasn't just about skirt lengths but a new social order. The new designers reflected this; they were the most modern, John Bates in particular."

Marit Allen
fashion editor

Bates's dress was chosen as dress of the year by the Fashion Museum in 1965.

Silver-foil tank dress
Betsey Johnson
1965

Plastic-insert knit minidress
Rudi Gernreich
1967

Disk Dress 1966

Paco Rabanne

Rabanne brought the precision of his industrial design background to his first fashion collection in 1966. The simple sleeveless minidress, shaped like an elongated vest, is composed of rigid disks of rhodoid—a cellulose acetate plastic—held together by metallic rings, which produces a chain mail effect (left). The dress was made using metal cutters, pliers, and a blowtorch, rather than a sewing machine and thread. The disks are positioned to create an interlocking herringbone pattern.

Prompted by the era of the space age, during which Yuri Gagarin became the first man in space in 1961, futuristic fashion featured new materials, including high-tech synthetic fabrics, and new methods of garment construction. Paco Rabanne eschewed classic couture techniques and pioneered the use of recycled materials, experimenting with fluorescent leather and fiberglass, knitted fur, and aluminum jersey, even producing paper dresses in 1967. He patented the Giffo process in 1968, in which all the component parts of a garment, including buttons, are molded in one piece, an innovation that established Rabanne as a fashion revolutionary.

> *The effect was breathtaking. Out strode the model, clothed in nothing but wafer-thin plastic disks, each glinting with dazzling sun colors and hung together with fine wires."*
>
> **Time magazine**

A radical new look symbolizes youth and optimism for the future.

Molded bustier
Issey Miyake
1983

Fastskin swimsuit
Speedo
2004

"I was very lucky, I was part of the postwar period when everything had to be redone. Women wanted to party, to dance, to amuse themselves; there was a sexy side."

Pierre Cardin

Cardin combines patent vinyl with space-age tabards in a futuristic collection.

Tabard Dress 1968
Pierre Cardin

Pierre Cardin attempted to fuse fashion with science, and to spearhead the notion of unisex clothes, with his first "Space Age" or "Cosmo Corps" collection in 1963. More commercial ranges followed, comprising pinafore dresses with stylized floral cutouts worn over skinny-rib jumpers and matching ribbed tights. Here, Cardin rationalizes the relationship of the constructed garment to the natural forms of the body by combining futuristic elements—modular-shaped metal buckles and thigh-high vinyl boots—with tabardlike minidresses, evidence of his modernist principles. The boots have a contemporary Cuban heel, and an ankle zip ensures a close fit, whereas the helmet is a compulsory component of Cardin's futuristic vision. The designer went on to develop an interest in man-made fibers, including Cardine, invented in 1968, an uncrushable fabric of bonded fibers that retains raised geometric forms in complex patterns.

The hard-edged, sculpted tabard shares out equal amounts of black and burnt orange, the latter forming the body of the dress, which is bisected by a broad, black belt with an outsize metallic buckle. Matching over-the-elbow PVC gloves feature a diamond motif on the hand and are bound in black. Elsewhere, bright blocks of color—lime, orange, and scarlet—are used to outline pockets, provide contrast at the hem, and to construct geometric yokes of space age-inspired motifs.

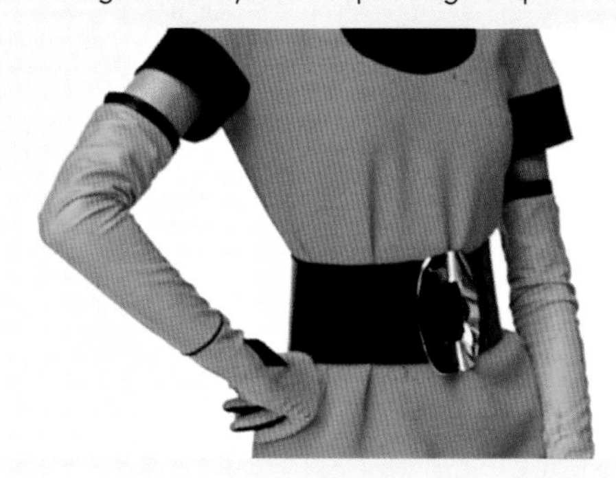

PVC coat
Mary Quant
1963

Silver-foil tank dress
Betsey Johnson
1965

Swarovski crystal minidress
Balmain
2009

Minidress of cutout circles
Roland Mouret
2010

Flying Saucer Dress

Issey Miyake 1994

Swaying in contrast to the movement of the wearer, the rolling disks of the flying saucer dress can be compressed or extended, thereby changing the width of the bands of color from narrow to broad. Paired in complementary colors, the pleating is imposed after the form is cut by enclosing the woven cloth between pre-folded card that radially compresses the polyester into permanent pleats when set with heat and pressure. Easily portable, the dress collapses into a single disk when not worn.

Freeing the body from the constraints of practicality and the need to seduce, the "flying saucer" dress is part of Issey Miyake's "Pleats Please" garment collection. The name makes reference to the flat-pack disk form of the dress, which resembles the collapsed accordion rings of a paper lantern. Miyake was inspired by the flexible light sculptures of his mentor, U.S. sculptor Isamu Noguchi. Whereas Noguchi encloses and diffuses light within folding veined structures, Miyake similarly contains the body within flexible, ridged textile forms that transmit and amplify gesture and motion with radially pleated surfaces of glossy polyester in vibrant hues.

"When the inside [of clothing] is as pleasing as the outside, what you have is couture. But when the inside is more important than that, what you have is Issey Miyake."

Georgina Howell
journalist

Miyake experiments with innovative techniques and novel garment forms.

Staircase dress
Issey Miyake
1994

Jacket
Junya Watanabe for Commes des Garçons 2008

"I feel the work is never done. I can recognize there is amazing work in my collections, but I usually see my pieces as prototypes for further development. After every project and collection is finished, I can always spot things that could have been improved."

Hussein Chalayan

The aeronautically engineered "monumental" dress relies on radical technical processes.

Airplane Dress 2000
Hussein Chalayan

Exploring the body's natural capacity for speed and the ways in which mobility can be enhanced by mechanical means, Hussein Chalayan juxtaposed the organic with the inorganic, and technology with the human form, in a series of three "monumental" dresses. They were named by the designer as "monuments to ideas" because of their carapacelike structure. Using technology from the aircraft industry and in collaboration with industrial designer Paul Topen, Chalayan worked on garments formed of a composite material created from glass fiber and resin, which was cast in specially designed molds. The dresses were exhibited at London's Sadler's Wells Theatre on a white set inspired by Constructivism, a movement that favored art as a practice for social purposes, which heralded the birth of early twentieth-century modernism. The resin garments were shown alongside "softer," more wearable designs constructed from cloth.

Operated mechanically by remote control, the mobile rear section and side flaps of the resin garment are raised and lowered like the wings of an airplane. Once the wings are open, layers of densely packed tulle are exposed. When they are closed, the garment reverts to its original aerodynamic form. The use of pale pink for the froufrou inserts further distances the frills from the hard-edged components that make up the dress. The rigid hem dips at the front, creating a swanlike silhouette.

Molded bustier
Issey Miyake
1983

Secret dress
Yohji Yamamoto
1999

Digital modern lighting dress
Junya Watanabe
2001

Long Live the Immaterial collection
Viktor & Rolf 2007

Bronze Dress 2012

Iris van Herpen

As a guest member of the Chambre Syndicale de la Haute Couture since 2011, van Herpen commands an establishment audience for the complex confections that wreath her models in her dreams of art, architecture, and science future. The plunging décolleté molded to the body and the pencil skirt, tipping the knee, attest to some adherence to dress code significance; all else has the alien power of a chrysalis in the process of metamorphosis, drawing the eye to voluptuous curves of faceted surface.

With elements of extraterrestrial theatricality, Iris van Herpen engages with the frontiers of material invention, fusing painstaking atelier traditions and spectacular sculptural experimentation. The garment is fabricated into its three-dimensional involute form from finely segmented, transparent plastic that has the sheen of bronze. Creating toothed bands that hold a radius rather than a fold, the flexing bonded ribbons are anchored edge to edge or overlapped to delineate the contours and fluid volume of the piece, which interacts with the wearer with a ponderous grace. The segmentation of the exoskeleton has the visual character of a soft-sculpted crustacean.

“*By bringing form, structure, and materials together in a new manner, I try to suggest and realize optimal tension and movement.*”

Iris van Herpen

A shifting lustrous surface forms a true carapace with the gloss of tortoiseshell.

Inflated PVC jacket
Gareth Pugh
2006

Wired dress
Pierre Cardin
2009

"Women can follow fashion too closely. I design for women who are content not to overstate their importance in the world or pose as princesses or ball-breakers."

Giorgio Armani

With a meticulous attention to form and finish in pastel colors, Armani provides contemporary tailoring.

Pastel Shell Ensemble 2012
Armani Privé

A legendary perfectionist with an uncompromising attitude to extraneous decoration, Giorgio Armani has turned understatement into his signature style. Removing any obvious understructure, the designer creates a smooth, modular silhouette by merely manipulating the fabric—a high-quality, three-ply silk cady, with a dense, soft shine—which was originally produced in the French region of Languedoc specifically for the couture trade. Evidence of the contemporary trend for head-to-toe color, the full palazzo pants are in the same soft pastels as the top, and fall in unpressed pleats from a narrow, high, shaped waistband, with vertical pockets set into each side seam.

Armani replaces the tailored trouser suit with his modernist version of shell top and trousers, both underpinned by a subtly exaggerated silhouette. The bodice is cut in two, the ellipse of the torso exactly matching the curve of the outer shoulder. The bias-cut, raglan-sleeved yoke has the liquidity of a knitted jersey: cut all in one, the sleeves pool in soft folds at the elbow. The perfection of the silhouette, which not only recognizes the body but also provides a carapace, is the result of a subtle mounting or lamination of the cloth. Hidden zips at the underarm provide a close fit.

Ombré cotton coat
Dries van Noten
2011

White jumpsuit
Céline
2011

Cropped viscose top and skirt
Chanel
2013

Pale gray oversized coat
Stella McCartney
2013

> *"It's all about dissection, tension, and subtraction expressed through structure and fluidity. We wanted the garments to float on the girls, but not in an ethereal way, always keeping the structure."*
>
> **Alexander Wang**

Airy expansion panels of Surrealist graphic legibility seem to float on the surface of the body.

Structured Top and Skirt 2013
Alexander Wang

With the precision of a draftsman plotting the exploded views of a self-assembly blueprint, Alexander Wang pursues fragmentation and construction that not only recalls André Courrèges but also references the articulation of the kinetic surfaces of an aircraft. Wang deploys a variety of skins in a complex structure: the lambskin skirt resting on the prow of the hips features figured eyelet embroidery, creating a mock-croc effect. Cropped to above the waist, the sectional silk halter is embroidered in reptilian detail and floats on a mesh of monofilament. The illusory theme of free-moving segmentation leads to an extended T-strap sandal in calfskin, harnessed below the knee.

Wang rarely detracts from the core narrative identity of his fluid, softly structured collections with extraneous color. Here he makes a theatrical exception with certain embroidery threads and base cloths, which fluoresce in glow shades under UV black light. The eyelet embroidery of the leather pencil skirt is revealed as an eerie, fluo-blue figurative contrast, and the white silk embroidered textile shows up only in the midnight of ultraviolet. All daylight illusion resides in the invisible attachments between the geometric fragments of fabric that hang mysteriously as garment units moving in unison.

Dress with cutaway sleeves
André Courrèges
1965

Disk dress
Paco Rabanne
1966

White blouse and skirt
Bottega Veneta
2012

Transparent organza jacket and skirt
Christopher Kane 2013

Christian Lacroix oversees the dressmaking skills of Jeanine Ouvrard for his debut collection in Paris (1987).

Adidas

The largest sportswear manufacturer in Europe and the second biggest sportswear manufacturer in the world, Adidas was founded in 1924 by Adolf Dassler and registered as a company in 1949, with headquarters in Herzogenaurach, Germany. Adidas is the parent company of the Adidas Group, which comprises Reebok sportswear company, TaylorMade-Adidas Golf company, and Rockport. During the late 1990s, Adidas divided the brand into three main groups: Adidas Performance, for the professional athlete; Adidas Originals, focusing on fashion; and Style Essentials, of which the main group is Y-3, by Yohji Yamamoto. Three parallel stripes of the official logo feature on all Adidas clothing and shoe designs.

» *A-15 Tracksuit* **p.117**

Adrian

Born in Connecticut, Adrian Adolph Greenberg (1903–59), better known as "Adrian," was appointed chief costume designer for Hollywood studios Metro-Goldwyn-Mayer in 1928. During his career, he designed costumes for more than 250 films, including gowns for the all-female cast of *The Women* (1939), which featured a ten-minute fashion parade of his designs, thus disseminating them to a wider audience, and *The Wizard of Oz* (1939). Adrian also worked with Hollywood luminaries such as Greta Garbo, Jean Harlow, Katharine Hepburn, Lana Turner, and Joan Crawford, for whom he designed the influential wide-shouldered silhouette. He left MGM in 1941 and set up his own independent fashion house the following year.

» *Tailored Suit* **p.161**

Alexander McQueen

After apprenticeships in Savile Row with bespoke tailors Anderson & Sheppard and subsequently Gieves & Hawkes, British-born Alexander McQueen (1969–2010) worked briefly with Japanese designer Koji Tatsuno and then Romeo Gigli in Milan. He graduated from Central Saint Martins College of Arts and Design in 1992, when his entire collection was bought by influential stylist Isabella Blow. From 1996 to 2001, McQueen acted as chief designer at couture house Givenchy. His work has been recognized with numerous awards, including British Designer of the Year, which he won four times. The label is now under the creative direction of his long-term assistant Sarah Burton.

» *Feather Dress* **p.29**
» *Highland Rape Collection* **p.99**
» *Corset* **p.135**

Alexander Wang

Born and raised in San Francisco, Chinese-American designer Alexander Wang studied fashion design at Parsons The New School for Design in New York and launched his own ready-to-wear label in 2007. His relaxed aesthetic of slouchy layers is underpinned by sportswear influences, and the T by Alexander Wang label comprises variations on the basic fashion T-shirt. In 2008, Wang won the *Vogue*/Council of Fashion Designers of America Fashion Fund, followed by the Swarovski Womenswear Designer of the Year in 2009. The designer introduced his first menswear collection in 2010. In 2012, he was appointed as the successor to Nicolas Ghesquière, creative head of French couture house Balenciaga.

» *Structured Top and Skirt* **p.193**

Altuzarra

Altuzarra is the eponymous label of French-born designer Joseph Altuzarra (1983–), and, since its debut collection of 2009, it has proved both a critical and commercial success. An alumnus of Marc Jacobs, Givenchy, and Proenza Schouler, as well as renowned pattern maker Nicolas Caito, Altuzarra launched his label after a period of working directly under Riccardo Tisci at Givenchy. Altuzarra shares a core aesthetic with the better-known house, focusing on an attention to pattern-cutting detail and textural interest. Early collections provided refined tailored wear, but the label has developed a more relaxed, grunge-inspired aesthetic since 2011, with the designer experimenting with new silhouettes and materials.

⊠ *Parka* **p.119**

Armani

Italian-born designer Giorgio Armani (1934–) has continued to evolve his signature minimalism since the inauguration of his label in 1974. The designer is now the sole shareholder of a business estimated at $7 billion. Armani revolutionized menswear in the 1980s by deconstructing the jacket, providing a loose, fluid silhouette. He applied the same minimalistic techniques to womenswear, using fabrics that draped around the body in shades of taupe, beige, and navy. Internationally known lines include Giorgio Armani, Emporio Armani, Armani Jeans, and Armani Exchange. Armani Privé is the most recent addition: a couture collection that is painstakingly made by hand in exquisite fabrics for red-carpet events.

⊠ *Pastel Shell Ensemble* **p.191**

Amaya Arzuaga

Having begun her career at her parents' knitwear label Elipse, Amaya Arzuaga (1970–) launched her own label in 1994. Most popular in her native Spain, she is renowned for creating sculptured garments with bold blocks of color that are both novel and wearable. A key feature of each collection is the adherence to the idea of asymmetry and volume, with sculptural shapes formed out of silk, cotton, viscose, and Lycra. Arzuaga also uses modern man-made fabrics, such as polyurethane and plastic, to dramatic sculptural effect. Pattern makes a rare appearance, and there is a clear preference for simplicity of line and form. The label includes accessories, menswear, swimwear, and home furnishings.

⊠ *Pierrot Ensemble* **p.167**

A B

Balenciaga

From 1937 to 1967, Cristóbal Balenciaga (1895–1972) reigned supreme as master couturier at one of the most revered fashion houses. It originated in a small atelier in San Sebastián, Spain, before Balenciaga opened his couture house in 1937, on avenue George V in Paris. There he experimented with cut and structure rooted in an austere architectural aesthetic. During the 1950s, he created a new silhouette, relinquishing the waist to produce the influential sack dress in 1957. In 1986, Jacques Bogart S.A. purchased and relaunched the brand, and in 1997 Nicolas Ghesquière became head designer. In 2001, the Gucci Group acquired the house, and in 2012 Alexander Wang was appointed as creative head.

» *Evening Dress* **p.129**

Bill Gibb

A self-confessed fashion romantic, Scottish-born William Elphinstone Gibb (1943–88) moved to London in 1962 to study at the then Saint Martins School of Art and the Royal College of Art. In 1966, he founded the boutique Alice Paul, before working as a freelance designer for London manufacturer Baccarat from 1969 to 1972, when he launched Bill Gibb Ltd. with his business partner Kate Franklin. He opened his first independent shop in London's Bond Street in 1975. Renowned for his complex use of polychromatic print and intricate embellishment of evening dresses, Gibb was awarded *Vogue* Designer of the Year in 1970 and became a Fellow of the Society of Industrial Artists and Designers, London, in 1975.

» *Multipatterned Dress and Jacket* **p.147**

Bottega Veneta

Luxury leather goods label Bottega Veneta was founded in 1966 by Michele Taddei and Renzo Zengiaro in the Veneta region of northeast Italy. (Bottega Veneta means "Venetian workshop.") British designer Giles Deacon and international fashion stylist Katie Grand fronted the brand in 1998, resulting in a more fashion-led profile. The company was subsequently acquired by the Gucci Group in 2001, and Deacon was replaced by German-born designer Tomas Maier. Bottega Veneta presented its first women's ready-to-wear runway show in 2005 and its first men's runway show in 2006. Additions to the brand include jewelry, eyewear, fragrances, and furniture, as well as traditional leather goods.

» *White Dress* **p.77**
» *Tea Dress* **p.157**

Burberry

One of Britain's oldest clothing manufacturers, Burberry was founded in 1856 by dressmaker Thomas Burberry. In 1880, he invented gabardine, a water-resistant cloth used for the production of the now iconic trench coat, and in 1891 the company opened its first London store. The signature camel, red, black, and white Burberry check was introduced as a lining for the trench coat in 1924. Yorkshire-born Christopher Bailey (1971–) brought the brand into the twenty-first century when he was appointed creative director of the label in 2001, transforming Burberry into one of the most celebrated international fashion labels. In 2009, he was named Designer of the Year at the British Fashion Awards.

» *Trench Coat* **p.107**

Celia Birtwell and Ossie Clark

Textile designer Celia Birtwell (1941–) and fashion designer Raymond "Ossie" Clark (1942–96) first met in the Cona Coffee Bar in Manchester. The couple moved to London, where Clark graduated from the Royal College of Art with a first-class degree in 1965. The following year, the duo collaborated on a collection for Quorum, an exclusive London boutique owned by the designer Alice Pollock. The label sold to international celebrities and 1960s luminaries such as the Rolling Stones, the Beatles, Marianne Faithfull, Bianca Jagger, Verushka, and Talitha Getty. Quorum was sold to British fashion house Radley, which introduced the Ossie Clark for Radley diffusion line in 1967.

» *Handkerchief Point Dress* **p.145**

Chanel

One of the most influential designers of the twentieth century, Gabrielle "Coco" Chanel (1883–1971) revolutionized women's dress with easy-to-wear clothes that epitomized modern simplicity. From a small atelier making "off the peg" clothes, Chanel established a reputation that enabled her to open her Parisian couture house in rue Cambon in 1918. Chanel popularized the three-piece cardigan suit in fluid jersey, the cornerstone of daytime fashion in the 1920s and 1930s. She closed her fashion house when war broke out in 1939 and did not reopen it until 1954, specializing in simply tailored suits. Chanel continued to design until her death in 1971. In 1983, German-born Karl Lagerfeld was appointed as artistic director of Chanel.

» *Skirt Suit* **p.41**
» *Little Black Dress* **p.71**

Charles James

British-born Charles James (1906–78) was a volatile but masterly couturier. He opened the first of his hat shops in Chicago, and later relocated to New York before moving to London in 1929, where he opened his first couture salon. Moving between Paris, London, and New York throughout the 1930s, James held his first fashion show in Paris in 1937. He continued to rework many of the designs from this period in subsequent collections, including the four-leaf clover or abstract gown. During the 1950s, the designer spent most of his time in New York, devoted to pursuing the perfect cut of a sleeve. With an engineer's interest in construction, he had little regard for commercial considerations. James retired in 1958.

» *Four-Leaf Clover Ball Gown* **p.17**

Christian Lacroix

Born in Arles, France, Christian Lacroix (1951–) developed a love of drawing and fashion, which, combined with fortuitous social connections, led to his position as head designer at the couture House of Patou in 1981. Considered the direct heir to Christian Dior, he opened his eponymous couture house in Paris in 1987 backed by entrepreneurs Jean-Jacques Picart and Bernard Arnault, reinvigorating the notion of couture with the extravagant sensuality of his first groundbreaking collection. Although enormously influential, the house never made a profit. In 2005, Arnault sold it to a U.S. company called the Falic Group, which filed for voluntary bankruptcy in 2009, resulting in Lacroix losing control of the house that bears his name.

» *Pouf Skirt* **p.151**

Commes des Garçons

Resolutely averse to the superficiality of fashion trends, Japanese designer Rei Kawakubo (1942–) established the Comme des Garçons (like the boys) label in 1973, having first adopted the name in 1969. A fine arts and literature graduate of Keio University in Tokyo, Kawakubo initially worked in a public relations role with Asahi Chemicals Industry, but left to become a freelance stylist. She opened her first boutique in Tokyo in 1975, and in 1981 she launched her first women's collection in Paris, where her uncompromising aesthetic won her international fashion acclaim. The designer won the first of two Mainichi Fashion Awards in 1983, and the Veuve Clicquot Business Woman of the Year Award in 1991.

» *Lace Sweater* **p.73**

Dior

A name synonymous with fashion, Christian Dior (1905–57) launched his eponymous couture house with the "New Look" in 1947. Funded by textile magnate Marcel Boussac, Dior created a furor with his lavish use of textiles after the austerity of World War II. This was followed by equally influential silhouettes, including the Ligne H in 1954 and the Ligne A in 1955. On Dior's untimely death, the twenty-one-year-old Yves Saint Laurent produced his first collection for the label. He was succeeded by Marc Bohan until 1989, when he was replaced by Italian designer Gianfranco Ferré and in 1996 by British designer John Galliano. Owned by Bernard Arnault of the LVMH luxury goods group, Dior now has Raf Simons as creative head.

⊠ *Le Bar Suit* **p.37**

Donna Karan

U.S. designer Donna Karan (1948–) studied at Parsons The New School for Design in New York, then worked for fellow American Anne Klein. Karan launched her eponymous brand with her then husband Stephan Weiss and the Takihyo Corporation in 1984, and the following year introduced her capsule collection, "Seven Easy Pieces." With an unerring eye for the fashion needs of the professional woman, Karan offers casual glamour and relaxed daywear, often in experimental fibers and fabrics. The diffusion line DKNY was launched in 1989. The designer has been recognized seven times by the Council of Fashion Designers of America, including a Lifetime Achievement Award in 2004. The brand is now owned by LVMH.

⊠ *Leotard* **p.115**

Elie Saab

Renowned for his luxurious red-carpet gowns, Lebanese-born Elie Saab (1964–) had no formal fashion training and launched his Beirut-based fashion label in 1982, when he was eighteen years old. In 1997, Saab became the first non-Italian designer to become a member of the Camera Nazionale della Moda, and in 1997 the designer showed his first collection outside Lebanon, in Rome. Saab gained international recognition in 2002, when he became the first Lebanese designer to dress an Academy Award winner, Halle Berry. In May 2003, the Chambre Syndicale de la Haute Couture invited him to become a member, and he showed his first haute couture collection in Paris in July 2003.

⊠ *Lace Dress* **p.139**

Fortuny

An inventor of revolutionary fabrics, textile artist Mariano Fortuny y Madrazo (1871–1949) was born in Spain, but is most closely associated with Venice, where he lived and worked for most of his life. Borrowing from ancient Greek forms, he utilized an innovative pleating technique, patented in 1909, for one of his most notable achievements: the Delphos gown. Fortuny manipulated cloth through printed and applied methods, with many processes frequently applied to a single length, combining color effects with stenciling and beading. In 1922, the designer established Fortuny, Inc. in collaboration with interior designer Elsie Lee McNeill. After his death, garments were no longer produced.

⊠ *Delphos Pleated Dress* **p.125**

Givenchy

One of the most influential couturiers of the mid-twentieth century and a favorite of Jackie Kennedy, wife of U.S. President John F. Kennedy, Hubert de Givenchy (1927–) opened the House of Givenchy in 1952. Two years later, he presented a range of luxury women's ready-to-wear. International acclaim followed, with costume designs for Audrey Hepburn in *Funny Face* (1957) and *Breakfast at Tiffany's* (1961). In 1988, Givenchy sold his business to LVMH, and the designer retired from fashion design in 1995. John Galliano assumed creative directorship of the house in 1995, followed by Alexander McQueen in 1996, and from 2001 to 2004 Julien Macdonald took the helm. Riccardo Tisci has been creative director of the house since 2005.

⊠ *Sack Dress* **p.43**

Hedi Slimane

Providing the paradigm for the new male ideal throughout the 2000s, Paris-born Italian-Tunisian designer Hedi Slimane (1968–) sent androgynous, wraithlike boys down the runway. After studying art history at the Ecole du Louvre, Slimane came to the attention of Pierre Bergé, longtime partner of Yves Saint Laurent and then chief executive of Yves Saint Laurent. Bergé hired Slimane for the Saint Laurent menswear design team in 1996, despite his lack of formal training. When the label was acquired by the Gucci Group in 1999, Slimane moved to Dior, unveiling his first collection for Dior Homme in 2001. Returning to Yves Saint Laurent as creative director in 2012, he rebranded the label Saint Laurent Paris.

⊠ *Two-piece Slimline Suit* **p.75**

Helen Rose

Foremost female Hollywood costumier Helen Rose (1904–85) was born in Chicago, where she studied at the Chicago Academy of Fine Arts. She moved to Los Angeles in 1929, where she designed skating outfits for the Ice Follies before joining Twentieth Century Fox film studios. In 1943, she moved to Metro-Goldwyn-Mayer, where she became head of design. Rose won two Academy Awards for Best Costume Design, for *The Bad and the Beautiful* in 1952 and *I'll Cry Tomorrow* in 1955. She often adapted her film designs for ready-to-wear, and popularized the sweetheart line with a strapless sheath for Elizabeth Taylor in *Cat on a Hot Tin Roof* (1958). In the late 1960s, Rose left the studio to open her own design business.

» *Wedding Dress of Princess Grace* **p.19**

Hermès

Thierry Hermès first opened a horse harness workshop in 1837 in the Grands Boulevard quarter of Paris, moving to 24 rue du Faubourg Saint-Honoré in 1880, when Charles-Emile Hermès purchased the building that still houses the flagship store and workshops. The company branched out and produced its first bag, the *haut à courroies*, in 1900. Hermès's first women's couture collection was shown in Paris in 1929. From 1956, ready-to-wear collections were designed by practitioners, including Martin Margiela from 1997 to 2003, Jean Paul Gaultier from 2003 until 2010, and Christophe Lemaire, whose first collection debuted in March 2011. In 2010, luxury goods company LVMH acquired a stake in the company.

» *Orange Suede and Paisley Ensemble* **p.23**

Hussein Chalayan

Intellectually challenging, Turkish-Cypriot fashion designer Hussein Chalayan (1970–) graduated from London's Central Saint Martins College of Arts and Design in 1993. Since then, the designer has been affiliated with a number of companies in addition to designing for his own label. From 1998 to 2001, he fronted the New York knitwear company TSE. This was followed by his appointment in 2001 as fashion director to the jeweler Asprey of London. Chalayan has won numerous accolades, including British Designer of the Year in 1999 and 2000, and the Design Star Honoree Award in New York in 2007. He has also collaborated with Puma sportswear, Swarovski, the Falke legwear label, and New York denim label J Brand.

» *Airplane Dress* **p.187**

Iris van Herpen

Iris van Herpen (1984–) studied fashion design at Artez Institute of the Arts Arnhem, graduating in 2006, followed by an internship at Alexander McQueen in London and Claudy Jongstra in Amsterdam. In 2011, she was invited to become a guest member of the Chambre Syndicale de la Haute Couture. Utilizing innovative and complex material and processes, including three-dimensional printing, she is known for creating avant-garde garments worn by celebrities, such as Lady Gaga, and for her numerous collaborations with artists from other disciplines, including, most notably, Bjork (whose stage costumes van Herpen designed in 2012). She has been designing her own label clothes since 2007.

» *Bronze Dress* **p.189**

I Was Lord Kitchener's Valet

At the epicenter of the "Swinging Sixties," retail emporium I Was Lord Kitchener's Valet opened in 1966 on London's Portobello Road. Ian Fisk and John Paul purveyed vintage military costume and Victorian memorabilia to the city's demi-monde and pop stars, including Mick Jagger and Jimi Hendrix. The following summer, Fisk and Paul dissolved their partnership, and Fisk took sole ownership of the premises. Paul and Robert Orbach opened a new branch of Kitchener's on Foubert's Place, selling militaria and novelty items. In 1966, Orbach added two more Kitchener's outlets, on Carnaby Street and Wardour Street, and soon expanded to sites in Piccadilly Circus and King's Road.

» *Union Jack Jacket* **p.143**

Irving Schott

U.S. clothing company Schott NYC was founded in 1913 by brothers Irving and Jack Schott and manufactured coats and jackets. Renowned for producing the first leather motorcycle jacket in 1928, the Perfecto, the company was also commissioned by the U.S. military during World War II and supplied the "bomber" jacket and the naval wool "pea coat," which it still manufactures. Associated with disaffected youth, represented by James Dean and Marlon Brando in films such as *The Wild One* (1953), the Schott Perfecto® was also adopted by rock stars in the 1970s and 1980s, including The Ramones and Joan Jett. Schott NYC remains a family-owned company and produces the majority of its clothing in the United States.

» *Black Leather Motorcycle Jacket* **p.91**

Issey Miyake

Born in Hiroshima, Issey Miyake (1938–) studied at Tama Art University, Tokyo, then worked in Paris and New York before opening the Miyake Design Studio in Tokyo in 1970. Key concepts have included his cast acrylic torso from 1983, the "Pleats Please" collections launched in 1993, and the radical technology of the A-POC construct-your-own garment, which won the Mainichi Design Prize in 2003. The designer was also honored with the Praemium Imperiale for Sculpture in 2005, the culmination of four decades of his engagement with the fashion industry. In order to focus on research, Miyake handed over the design of the collections to Naoki Takizawa, who was replaced by Dai Fujiwara as creative director in 2007.

⨠ *Flying Saucer Dress* **p.185**

Jean Paul Gaultier

Notoriously irreverent French fashion designer Jean Paul Gaultier (1952–) was recruited as design assistant to Pierre Cardin at the age of seventeen on the strength of an unsolicited portfolio of sketches. Following experience at Jacques Esterel and the House of Patou, he launched his own label with a collection for Mayagor in 1976. From 1978 to 1981, Gaultier enjoyed backing from the Japanese conglomerate Kashiyama, and the Italian groups Gibo and Equator supported his woven and knitted manufacturing, respectively. In 2003, he became the creative director at Hermès until his resignation in 2010. Accolades include the International Award of the Council of Fashion Designers of America in 2000.

⨠ *Conical Bra Dress* **p.131**

Jil Sander

Immutable minimalist Jil Sander (1943–) graduated from the textile school in Krefeld near Hamburg and began her career as a freelance fashion designer in 1968, opening the first Jil Sander boutique the same year. Her first womenswear range was launched in 1973, and in 1978 she established Jil Sander as a limited liability company (GmbH). With the Lancaster Group in 1979, the designer launched cosmetics and fragrances: PURE woman and PURE man. In 1999, the Prada Group management took over Jil Sander AG, and in 2000 Sander resigned from the company, returning in 2003 for two collections. The designer withdrew once more from her own label but returned to her eponymous brand in 2012.

⨠ *Cutaway Top and Culottes* **p.85**

John Bates

British fashion innovator John Bates (1938–) apprenticed under Gerard Pipart at Herbert Sidon before launching his own label in 1959 under the name Jean Varon. One of the first designers to crop dresses to mid-thigh length, Bates produced influential designs that included bare midriffs, sheer panels and cutouts, and the use of modern materials such as metallic fabrics and PVC. In 1965, he designed the garments worn by actress Diana Rigg for her role as Emma Peel in the cult television show *The Avengers* (1961–69). These costumes included Op art-influenced monochrome outfits and accessories, and the first "hipster" trousers. The Fashion Museum, Bath, held a major retrospective show of the designer's work in 2006.

» *Casbah Dress* **p.179**

John Galliano

Although his groundbreaking graduation collection from Central Saint Martins College of Arts and Design was bought in its entirety by prestigious London store Browns in 1984, John Galliano (1960–) struggled to survive commercially under his own label. However, his unique aesthetic of romanticism and innovative tailoring led to his appointment by Bernard Arnault as head of the House of Givenchy in 1995, the first British designer to oversee a French haute couture house. Following his years as design director at Givenchy, in 1996 LVMH moved Galliano to Christian Dior, where he remained in the role of creative director until 2011. He has since worked for U.S. designer Oscar de la Renta.

» *Maria-Luisa Ball Gown* **p.153**
» *Strapless Gown* **p.163**

Kenzo

Renowned for juxtaposing layers of multipatterned textures, Japanese fashion designer Kenzo Takado (1939–) studied at Tokyo's Bunka Fashion College before moving to Paris in 1964. After a period working as a freelance designer, Kenzo opened his first boutique, Jungle Jap, in 1970. He produced his first menswear collection in 1983, and in 1988 a successful women's perfume line, Kenzo de Kenzo, was launched. In 1993, the label was bought by LVMH. Kenzo Takada announced his retirement in 1999, and in 2003 Italian designer Antonio Marras joined the brand and was appointed creative director in 2008, succeeded by Humberto Leon and Carol Lim, the duo behind cult U.S. clothing store Opening Ceremony.

» *Multipatterned Print and Knit Ensemble* **p.61**

Lanvin

Known for exquisite embellishment and appropriation of exotic influences, Jeanne Lanvin (1867–1946) trained as a milliner and dressmaker in Paris and Barcelona before opening her own Parisian millinery shop in 1889. She married an Italian noble, Emilio di Pietro, in 1895, with whom she had a daughter, Marguerite di Pietro. Lanvin developed her skills as a dressmaker and designer with her children's collection in 1908, and in 1909 joined the Chambre Syndicale de la Haute Couture. The House of Lanvin was formally founded in the early 1920s at 22 rue du Faubourg Saint-Honoré. Publishing magnate Shaw-Lan Wang bought a controlling interest in the house and appointed Alber Elbaz as artistic director in 2001.

⧐ *Robe de Style* **p.55**

Lee

Lee Jeans is a U.S. company that predominantly produces denim garments, most significantly fashion jeans. Established by Henry David Lee (1849–1928), the company (known as the Lee Mercantile Company) began manufacturing hard-wearing denim dungarees and jackets for working men in Salina, Kansas, in 1889. The small range of garments expanded to include an all-in-one jumpsuit in 1913 and an overall in 1920. The brand began to move into the casual street clothing market in 1954. This part of the company was consolidated in the 1970s when Lee emphasized its status as a fashion brand and branched out into womenswear and childrenswear. A key garment in the Lee brand is the Lee slim 101J, introduced in 1932.

⧐ *Blue Jeans* **p.113**

Louis Vuitton

Founder of the company now synonymous with luxury goods and a high-profile fashion label, Louis Vuitton (1821–92) began his career when he was appointed as *layetier,* or expert packer, to Empress Eugénie de Montijo. Maison Louis Vuitton opened in 1854, on rue Neuve-des-Capucines, Paris, where Vuitton began to design his own luggage. In 1987, the company merged with the champagne group Moët Hennessy, run by Bernard Arnault, to form one of the world's most powerful luxury goods conglomerates. Patrick Louis Vuitton, the great great grandson of the founder, is currently the president of the company. In 1997, U.S. designer Marc Jacobs was appointed to oversee the brand.

⧐ *Belle Epoque Ensemble* **p.67**

Madame Grès

Renowned for the classical drapery of her gowns, Germaine Emilie Krebs (1903–93), known as Alix Barton and later as "Madame Grès," began her career in fashion as a dressmaker. She also established her reputation as a costume designer before serving a brief apprenticeship at the couture House of Premet. In 1942, she opened her own design house in Paris under the name "Grès" (a partial anagram of her husband's first name, Serge). In 1972, Grès was elected president of the Chambre Syndicale de la Haute Couture, and four years later was awarded its highest honor: the Dé d'or. During the 1980s, Maison Grès fell into decline, and in 1986 the designer was expelled from the Chambre Syndicale for non-payment of dues.

» *Pleated Evening Dress* **p.39**

Maison Martin Margiela

Iconoclast and maverick Belgian designer Martin Margiela (1957–) studied at Antwerp's Royal Academy of Fine Arts alongside the experimental fashion collective the "Antwerp Six." He challenged the traditional notion of fashion as a commercial commodity by subverting the rational approach to garment construction. Margiela worked for Parisian couturier Jean Paul Gaultier between 1985 and 1987 before launching his own label in 1989. Despite his revolutionary approach to design, in 1997 he was hired by the traditional luxury house Hermès to energize the label. The Margiela brand was acquired by Diesel in 2002, after which the designer left the company, leaving his seventy-strong design team to carry on.

» *Organza Dress* **p.103**

Marc Jacobs

New York-born designer Marc Jacobs (1963–) studied at Parsons The New School For Design before launching his debut collection under his own name in 1986. The following year he became the youngest ever recipient of the Council of Fashion Designers of America (CFDA) Perry Ellis Award for New Fashion Talent. In 1989, Jacobs joined Perry Ellis as vice-principal of women's design and won the CFDA award for Women's Designer of the Year for his "Grunge" collection, before launching his own label in 1993. In 1997, luxury goods conglomerate LVMH appointed Jacobs as its artistic director for the company's first ready-to-wear range. The Marc by Marc Jacobs collection was introduced in 2001, together with an accessories line.

» *Striped Suit* **p.49**

Marchesa

With evening wear as its main focus, British brand Marchesa was launched in 2004 by Georgina Chapman (1976–) and Keren Craig (1976–). The design duo met while studying at Chelsea College of Art and Design in London. Chapman, a 2001 graduate of the Wimbledon College of Art, began her career as a theatrical costume designer before moving into high fashion. Craig graduated from Brighton School of Art in 2000 with a specialist interest in print and embroidery. Chapman's marriage to Hollywood mogul Harvey Weinstein has given the label access to A-list celebrities, and the gowns are frequently worn on the red carpet. In 2006, the less expensive diffusion line Notte By Marchesa was introduced.

⊠ *Art Nouveau Gown* **p.169**

Mary Katrantzou

In 2001, Athens-born Mary Katrantzou (1983–) left Greece to study architecture in Rhode Island, before moving to London to study textile design. Her postgraduate collection from Central Saint Martins College of Arts and Design was nominated for both the Harrods and the L'Oreal Professional awards. Katrantzou produced her first ready-to-wear collection of nine dresses for fall/winter 2008, and debuted at London Fashion Week through a British Fashion Council New Generation/Topshop sponsored stand. In 2009, the designer was awarded the New Generation sponsorship for six seasons, and in 2011 won the Emerging Talent Award – Ready-to-Wear at the British Fashion Awards.

⊠ *Jewel Tree Dress* **p.25**

Meadham Kirchhoff

Juxtaposing a saccharine palette with elements of schlock horror and historical pastiche, the Meadham Kirchhoff label is the brainchild of design duo Edward Meadham (1979–) and Benjamin Kirchhoff (1978–). Both graduates of Central Saint Martins College of Arts and Design, their first joint venture was a menswear line, Benjamin Kirchhoff, and it was not until they showed in 2006 that they adopted the united branding for their womenswear label. This won the Emerging Talent Award – Ready-to-Wear at the British Fashion Awards in 2010, and the duo was shortlisted for the British Fashion Council/*Vogue* Designer Fashion Fund 2012. In 2010, the label produced a diffusion range with high-street retailers Topshop.

⊠ *Embellished Tulle Dress* **p.171**

Michael Kors

The restrained yet sophisticated style of U.S. designer Michael Kors (1959–) has consistently provided luxurious essentials for the international market since the inception of the label in 1981. Kors was born Karl Anderson, on Long Island, and studied at the Fashion Institute of Technology in New York. Named the first ever creative director for a French fashion house, Céline, in 1997, Kors left the label in October 2003 to concentrate on his own brand, having launched a menswear line in 2002. Diffusion lines MICHAEL Michael Kors and KORS Michael Kors were launched in 2004. The designer has been the recipient of many awards, including the Geoffrey Beene Lifetime Achievement Award from the Council of Fashion Designers of America in 2010.

⊠ *Gothic Ensemble* **p.165**

Miu Miu

Miu Miu's signature idiosyncratic detailing and muted palette place the label in the category of the avant-garde, while retaining fashion-led credibility. Granddaughter of the founder of Prada, Miuccia Prada (1949–) studied political science before embarking on a career in fashion. In 1992, she created Miu Miu—the term is a childhood diminutive of her name—as a secondary "little sister" line to Prada in order to engage with a younger, more adventurous demographic. The first Miu Miu stores, in Paris and Milan, were joined by another in New York in 1996. Forty more have followed. Both labels showed in Milan until 2006, when Miu Miu moved to Paris to differentiate the contrasting aesthetic of the two labels.

⊠ *Denim Ensemble* **p.83**

Nicolas Ghesquière

With the exception of a period as an assistant to Jean Paul Gaultier and various freelance commissions, French-born Nicolas Ghesquière (1971–) was unknown when he began working at Balenciaga, designing golf outfits and mourning clothes, in 1995. When creative director Josephus Thimister departed in 1997, Ghesquière was promoted. In 2000, he was named Avant-Garde Designer of the Year at the VH1/*Vogue* Fashion Awards. The following year, Balenciaga was acquired by the Gucci Group, after which Ghesquière was given access to the Balenciaga archives, which previously had been tightly held. In 2012, the management wished to push the brand in a more commercial direction so Ghesquière left the label.

⊠ *Ruffled Skirt* **p.175**

Nicole Farhi

French-born designer Nicole Farhi (1946–), arbiter of relaxed, restrained fashion, trained as an illustrator at the Studio Berçot in Paris before designing garments for dressmaking patterns for magazines such as *Marie Claire* and *Elle*. She subsequently launched French Connection in the early 1970s with British fashion entrepreneur Stephen Marks, whom she later married. In 1982, Farhi launched her own label with the backing of Marks's company. The Farhi brand diversified into menswear in 1989, followed by shoes and accessories, swimwear, home furnishings, and evening wear. OpenGate capital bought the label in 2010, with Farhi remaining as creative director. She was awarded the Légion d'honneur the same year.

» *Gothic Ensemble* **p.165**

Paco Rabanne

Spanish-born Francisco "Paco" Rabaneda Cuervo is more commonly known as Paco Rabanne (1934–). The designer rejected traditional couture techniques and labeled his debut collection of 1966 "Twelve Unwearable Dresses in Contemporary Materials," which established him as a fashion iconoclast. Initially a jewelry designer, Rabanne brought his experience of working with rhodoid to his garments, and also developed new methods of assemblage. The commercial success of a series of perfumes, first launched in 1969 in collaboration with Spanish company Puig, has enabled the designer to continue his fashion experiments. A retrospective of his work was held at the Musée de la Mode in Marseille in 1995.

» *Disk Dress* **p.181**

Perry Ellis

Leading exponent of East Coast preppy style, U.S.-born Perry Ellis (1940–86) first graduated from the College of William and Mary in Williamsburg, Virginia, in 1961 with a degree in business administration, followed by a master's degree in retailing in 1963 from New York University. He gained experience as a buyer and merchandiser before launching his first women's sportswear line, Portfolio, in 1976, later founding his own fashion house, Perry Ellis International, in 1978. The company continued to expand throughout the 1980s, and in 1984 Perry Ellis America was created in collaboration with Levi Strauss. Ellis was presented with the Council of Fashion Designers of America Fashion Award in 1981.

» *Grunge Ensemble* **p.97**

Phoebe Philo for Céline

Under the aegis of Paris-born, British-based Phoebe Philo (1973–), Céline is one of the foremost influences in contemporary fashion. Originally founded in 1945 by Madame Céline Vipiana as a purveyor of children's shoes, and later expanded into the ready-to-wear women's clothing market, Céline was purchased by LVMH in 1996. The company appointed Phoebe Philo as creative director in 2008, and she presented her first collection for fall 2009. After graduating from Central Saint Martins College of Arts and Design in 1996, Philo worked as Stella McCartney's design assistant at French label Chloé before succeeding her as creative director in 2001. She fronted the label for five years and resigned in 2006.

⊠ *Leather Tunic* **p.79**

Pierre Cardin

Italian-born, French-based designer Pierre Cardin (1922–) challenged the fashion status quo by designing a ready-to-wear collection for Printemps department store in 1959, for which he was expelled from the ranks of haute couture practitioners. A former architecture student, the designer moved to Paris in 1945 where he worked with both Jeanne Paquin and Elsa Schiaparelli before heading to Christian Dior's tailleure atelier in 1946. Cardin founded his own house in 1950 and began his haute couture practice in 1953. From 1971, he showed his collections at his own venue: the Espace Cardin in Paris. In 1977, the designer received the first of three De d'or awards in recognition of his haute couture collections.

⊠ *Tabard Dress* **p.183**

Poiret

French-born Paul Poiret (1879–1944) injected vivid color combinations and exotic silhouettes into the ladylike pastels and "S"-shape corsets of the belle époque. After training with two major couturiers, Jacques Doucet and the House of Worth, Poiret founded his own maison de couture in 1903 on rue Auber, Paris. From 1906 to 1911, he presented garments that promoted an etiolated, high-waisted silhouette, but after seeing a production of *Scheherazade* by Les Ballets Russes in 1910, Poiret embraced his orientalist sensibilities, designing harem pantaloons and "lampshade" tunics for his collections. Such lavish extravagances failed to appeal during the modernism of the 1920s, resulting in the closure of his business in 1929.

⊠ *Robe Sorbet* **p.53**

Prada

In 1977, Muiccia Prada (1949–) took over the family business that had been founded by her grandfather, Mario, in 1913 as a purveyor of leather goods. She had her first commercial success a year later with the introduction of the much-imitated backpack, made from black Pocono industrial nylon with a discreet small triangular logo; it became the coveted accessory of the 1980s. Having launched collections of footwear and handbags, the designer presented her first women's ready-to-wear collection in 1989 in Milan. The Prada label has been further expanded through acquisitions, including Church & Co., a British footwear manufacturer, and designer brands such as Helmut Lang, Jil Sander, and Gucci.

» *Ombré Dress* **p.173**

Pringle

One of Britain's oldest heritage labels and now a high-fashion brand, luxury knitwear manufacturers Pringle of Scotland was founded by Robert Pringle in 1815. Initially, the company produced luxury hosiery, introducing cashmere in 1870, but Pringle is renowned for the creation in the 1920s of the intarsia design known as the Argyle pattern, which it revived in the 1950s for the Ryder Cup golf shirt. The brand became a public company in 1960. In 2000, Pringle was bought by the Hong Kong-based Fang brothers in a move to reinvigorate the label, aided by British designer Clare Waight Keller, the brand's creative director from 2005 until 2011. She was succeeded by ex-Balenciaga designer Alistair Carr.

» *Twinset* **p.111**

Pucci

Labeled the "prince of prints" by the U.S. press at the height of his fame, Emilio Pucci (1914–92) designed glamorous leisurewear for the newly mobile jet set. He launched his first fashion business on the isle of Capri, later moving to Rome and establishing headquarters in Florence. Pucci's use of vivid color and kaleidoscopic prints inspired both Stephen Sprouse and Gianni Versace. In 2000, the French luxury conglomerate LVMH bought a majority stake. In 2002, Christian Lacroix was appointed as artistic director, replaced by Matthew Williamson in 2005, followed by the current designer, Peter Dundas, in 2009. Laudomia Pucci, Emilio's daughter, is the current director of the Pucci fashion empire.

» *Caftan* **p.57**

Raf Simons

The most influential menswear designer of the 2000s and now bringing his austere yet seductive aesthetic to the heritage couture House of Dior, Belgian-born designer Raf Simons (1968–) graduated in 1991 with a degree in industrial and furniture design. He presented his first menswear collection in Milan in 1995, followed by his debut formal menswear show in Paris in 1997. In 2000, Simons was appointed head of the fashion department at the University of Applied Arts in Vienna, a position he held until 2005 when he was named creative director of Jil Sander mens- and womenswear. In 2012, LVMH announced that Simons was to replace John Galliano as creative head of Dior.

⊠ *Asymmetric Dress* **p.47**

Ralph Lauren

Exponent of aspirational lifestyle marketing and the embodiment of the American dream, Ralph Lauren (1939–) was born Ralph Rueben Lifshitz in the New York City borough of Bronx to an immigrant family. The designer's global fashion empire was founded in 1967 with his first tie shop, and he began designing menswear under the Polo Ralph Lauren label in 1969. In 1971, he introduced a womenswear label, and in 1972 he released the first mesh polo shirt, now an established preppy classic. The brand was floated on the U.S. stock market in 1997, with Lauren remaining the biggest shareholder. The label now includes Polo Ralph Lauren, Polo Sport, and the Ralph Lauren collection. He was awarded the Légion d'honneur in 2010.

⊠ *Coat Dress and Chaps* **p.63**
⊠ The Great Gatsby *Suit* **p.149**

Riccardo Tisci

Riccardo Tisci (1974–) made his debut at Givenchy in 2005 with an haute couture presentation at the fashion house's Paris headquarters, replacing the cool, sophisticated Givenchy aesthetic with a gothic-inspired romanticism. Born in the town of Taranto, in Puglia, Italy, the youngest of nine children, Tisci studied at the Art Institute of Cantù, Italy, before he moved to London, graduating from Central Saint Martins College of Arts and Design in 1999. He worked for Puma and Italian fashion label Coccapani, before establishing his own label in 2004. In 2005, he was unexpectedly appointed creative director of the French House of Givenchy by LVMH, surrendering his own line.

⊠ *Cate Blanchett's Dress* **p.27**

Roberto Cavalli

Projecting a brazenly seductive aesthetic, Florence-born designer Roberto Cavalli (1940–) exemplifies Italian fashion bravura. After his debut show at the Salon for Prêt-à-Porter in Paris in 1970, the designer opened his first boutique in Saint-Tropez in 1972, selling signature pieces of printed leather. In collaboration with his wife and business partner Eva Düringer since the early 1990s, the label has produced red-carpet showstoppers, usually featuring animal print. In 2009, Roberto Cavalli SpA and Ittierre SpA confirmed an exclusive worldwide licensing agreement for the production and distribution of Just Cavalli menswear, womenswear, apparel, bags, shoes, and accessories collections.

» *Animal Print Dress* **p.65**

Rodarte

Without any formal training, the Mulleavy sisters—Kate (1979–) and Laura (1980–)—produce complex otherworldly fantasy fashion under the label Rodarte, based in Pasadena, California. Their runway collections are conceptually led rather than commercial, with an idiosyncratic point of view based on their backgrounds in the liberal arts, combined with exquisite craftsmanship. In 2005, Rodarte attracted a number of industry awards and successfully collaborated with Gap and Target. In 2008, the sisters won the Swiss Textiles Award, the first women and non-Europeans to achieve this accolade. An exhibition, "Rodarte: States of Matter," opened at the Museum of Contemporary Art in Los Angeles in 2012.

» *Hand-crafted Dress* **p.101**

Roland Mouret

Although his training consisted of only three months in a Parisian fashion college, French designer Roland Mouret (1962–) launched his eponymous label in 1998 and made his debut at London Fashion Week the same year. Less than two months after the introduction of the iconic Galaxy dress in 2005, the designer abruptly resigned from the label following a dispute with the company's owners, Sharai and André Meyers, and lost the right to use his name commercially. Mouret cofounded a new company, 19RM, with Simon Fuller in 2006, and in 2010, he regained the right to use his full name. The same year he presented his first menswear collection. Debut shoe and bridal collections followed in 2012.

» *Galaxy Dress* **p.45**

Schiaparelli

Born to aristocratic parents at Palazzo Corsini in Rome, Elsa Schiaparelli (1890–1973) began her longtime association with the avant-garde when she moved to New York in 1919, where she met artists Marcel Duchamp and Man Ray. She returned to Paris in 1922 and worked freelance before launching her first collection in 1929 from her boutique in rue de la Paix. Schiaparelli achieved immediate success with her *trompe l'oeil* knitwear designs and expanded to offer a full range of clothing. From 1941 until the end of World War II, she lived in the United States, reopening her house in Paris in 1945. In 1954, the couturière closed her French fashion house and returned to New York to concentrate on designing costume jewelry.

» *Lobster Dress* **p.89**

Stella McCartney

Renowned for her sharp tailoring, British-born designer Stella McCartney (1971–) underwent a brief internship at couture house Christian Lacroix and a period working for Savile Row tailor Edward Sexton before studying at Central Saint Martins College of Arts and Design. Her appointment as creative director of French ready-to-wear house Chloé in 1997 followed two years after her graduation. McCartney left Chloé to launch her own label in 2001 under the umbrella of the Gucci Group. Accessories and fragrances followed, and, in 2007, an organic skincare line, CARE. McCartney put out a joint venture line with sportswear company Adidas in 2004, and in 2012 she designed the Olympics kit for Team Great Britain.

» *Jumpsuit* **p.121**

Tom Ford

Rebranding the Gucci label and resurrecting the double "G" logo in the 1990s, Texas-born Thomas Carlyle Ford (1962–) set the paradigm for fusing sex with fashion. Ford studied architecture at Parsons The New School for Design in New York, spending his final year studying fashion, before working for U.S. designer Cathy Hardwick and in 1998 for Perry Ellis. He was appointed by Dawn Mello, Gucci's creative director, as the brand's chief women's ready-to-wear designer in 1990, and in 1994 was promoted to creative director, pursuing the same role when Gucci acquired the House of Yves Saint Laurent in 1995. Ford temporarily retired from fashion in 2004 before introducing his own womenswear label in 2010.

» *Cutout Dress* **p.133**

Valentino

Synonymous with über-glamorous evening gowns for more than five decades, Valentino Garavani (1932–) studied at both L'Ecole des Beaux-Arts and L'Ecole de la Chambre Syndicale de la Couture Parisienne. He was apprenticed to Jacqueline de Ribes at Jean Dessès and later moved on to work for Guy Laroche, before returning to Rome to open his own small atelier in 1959. His international debut took place in 1962 in Palazzo Pitti, Florence, the Italian fashion capital of the time. The designer was inducted into the French Légion d'honneur in 2006. Valentino retired the following year, and the label is now fronted by Maria Grazia Chiuri and Pierpaolo Piccioli, who together had previously designed accessories for the brand.

⊠ *Rosso Valentino Evening Dress* **p.31**

Versace

Fashion maximalist Gianni Versace (1947–97) was born in the town of Reggio Calabria, Italy, and began his career in fashion in 1972 designing for Genny, Complice, and Callaghan. The first Versace boutique was opened in Milan's Via della Spiga in 1978, the same year that the designer launched his own label. In 1989, he opened the couture workshop Atelier Versace, and throughout the following decade he epitomized high-octane glamour for the super rich with extrovert body-enhancing gowns in his signature Mannerist prints. Versace launched Versus, a more youthful line, in 1990 under the directorship of his sister and muse, Donatella. After his death in 1997, she assumed creative directorship of the label.

⊠ *Pop Art Print Dress* **p.21**
⊠ *Bamboo Print Dress* **p.137**

Vionnet

French-born designer Madeleine Vionnet (1876–1975) created a new relationship between cloth and the body with the introduction of classically inspired gowns and innovative cutting techniques. After a period working for Callot Soeurs and Jacques Doucet in Paris, Vionnet first opened her salon at 222 rue de Rivoli in 1912, but closed it for the duration of World War I. In 1919, the designer began a twenty-year limited partnership under the name Madeleine Vionnet & Cie. She presented her final collection in 1939, when she was also awarded the Légion d'honneur. Resurrecting the brand in 2011, Italian twin sisters Barbara and Lucia Croce presented their first runway show in Paris.

⊠ *Bias-cut Evening Ensemble* **p.35**

Vivienne Westwood

Chief architect of the punk movement, Derbyshire-born Vivienne Westwood (1941–) worked as a teacher before opening a shop—Let it Rock, selling 1950s memorabilia—in 1971 with partner Malcolm McLaren. It was rebranded and renamed Too Fast to Live Too Young to Die in 1972, and reopened as SEX in 1974, purveying sado-masochistic bondage paraphernalia. Westwood launched her first solo collection, "Pirates," in 1981. The designer's global empire comprises the demi-couture line Gold Label, a ready-to-wear line Red Label, Vivienne Westwood Man, and the diffusion line Anglomania, which was introduced in 1997. Westwood was made a Dame of the British Empire in 2006 for services to fashion.

⧐ *Planet Gaia* **p.155**

Yohji Yamamoto

Japanese designer Yohji Yamamoto (1943–) graduated from Bunka Fashion College in 1969 and established his own line in Tokyo in 1972. From a first catwalk show of womenswear in Tokyo in 1977, the brand was expanded to include a menswear line in 1979 and the more experimental Yohji Yamamoto range in 1981, the same year that the designer showed in Paris for the first time, alongside fellow Japanese deconstructionalist Rei Kawakubo. In 1994, Yamamoto became the first Japanese fashion designer to be awarded the French Chevalier de L'Ordre des Arts et des Lettres. His ranges include Yohji Yamamoto, Yohji Yamamoto Pour Homme, Yohji Yamamoto + Noir, Y's, Y-3, and Y's for Living.

⧐ *White Shirt* **p.81**

Yves Saint Laurent

Pioneer of prêt-à-porter and fashion legend Yves Saint Laurent (1936–2008) was born in Oran, Algeria. He was appointed head designer of the House of Dior in 1957, successfully launching the "trapeze" line with his first collection. Conscripted to serve in the French army in 1960, Saint Laurent subsequently suffered a nervous breakdown. Following a period of convalescence, the designer and his partner, industrialist Pierre Bergé, launched their own fashion house in 1962. In 1966, the first of the company's Rive Gauche ready-to-wear stores opened on rue de Tournon in the 6th arrondissement of Paris. Saint Laurent retired in 2002 and was awarded the rank of Grand officier de la Légion d'honneur in 2007.

⧐ *Long Evening Ensemble* **p.59**
⧐ *Pinstripe Suit* **p.95**

TIMELINE

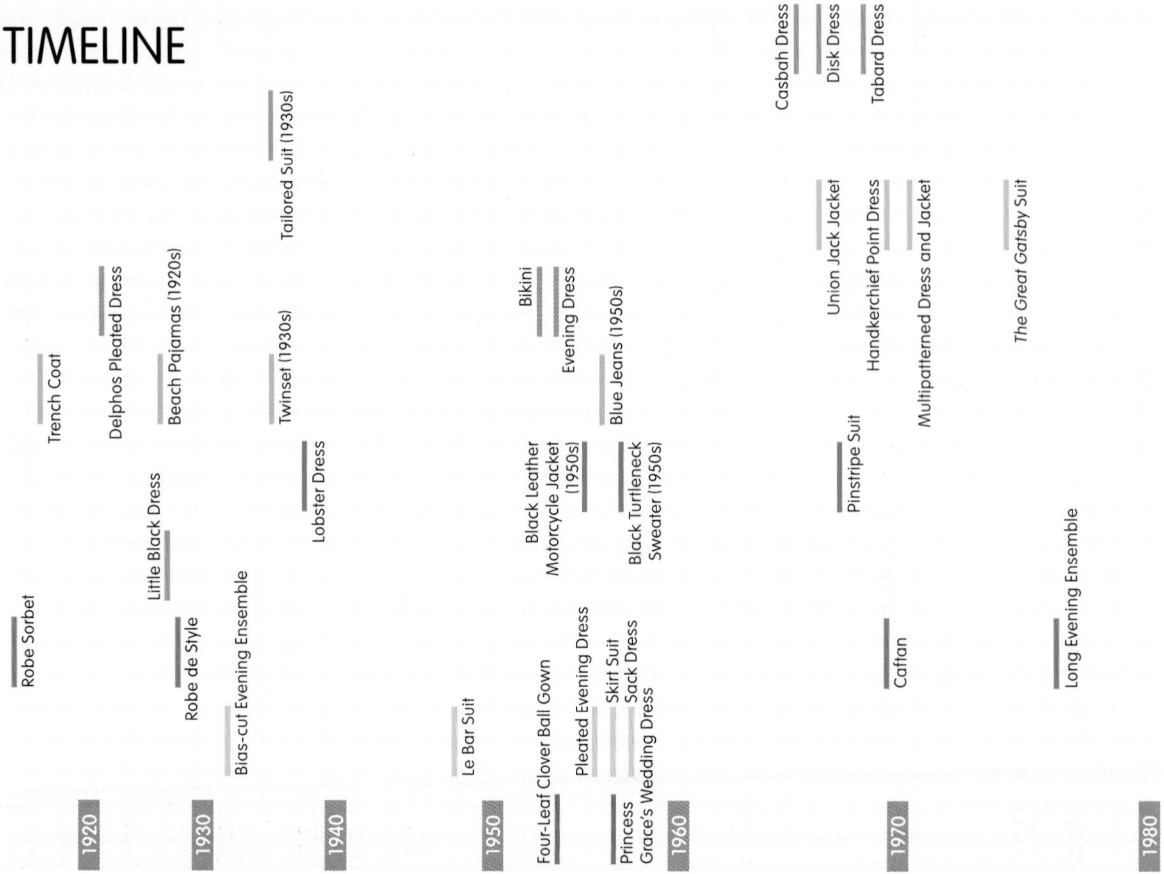

- Robe Sorbet
- Trench Coat

1920

- Delphos Pleated Dress
- Little Black Dress
- Beach Pajamas (1920s)
- Robe de Style

1930

- Bias-cut Evening Ensemble
- Tailored Suit (1930s)
- Twinset (1930s)
- Lobster Dress

1940

- Le Bar Suit

1950

- Bikini
- Black Leather Motorcycle Jacket (1950s)
- Four-Leaf Clover Ball Gown
- Evening Dress
- Pleated Evening Dress
- Blue Jeans (1950s)
- Skirt Suit
- Princess Grace's Wedding Dress
- Black Turtleneck Sweater (1950s)
- Sack Dress

1960

- Casbah Dress
- Disk Dress
- Union Jack Jacket
- Pinstripe Suit
- Tabard Dress
- Handkerchief Point Dress
- Caftan
- Multipatterned Dress and Jacket

1970

- *The Great Gatsby* Suit
- Long Evening Ensemble

1980

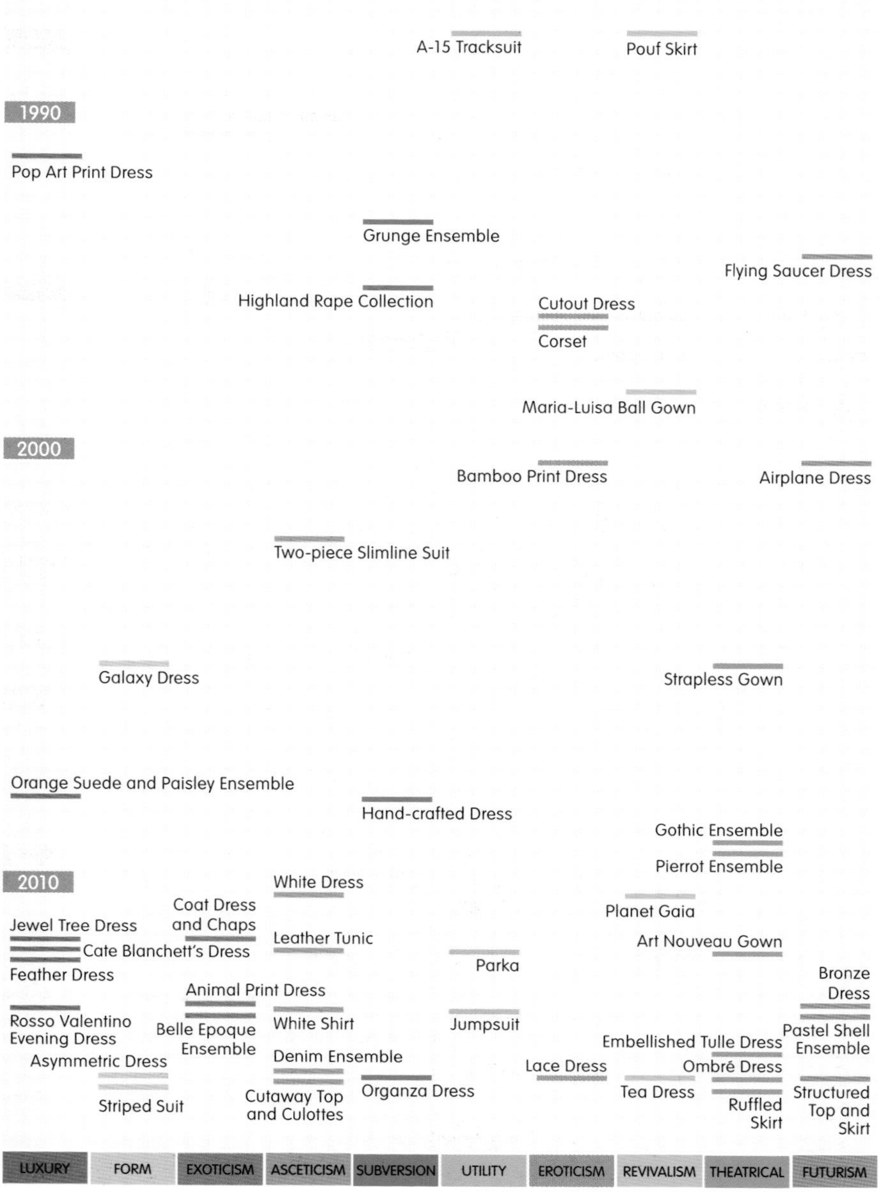

A-15 Tracksuit

Pouf Skirt

1990

Pop Art Print Dress

Grunge Ensemble

Flying Saucer Dress

Highland Rape Collection

Cutout Dress

Corset

Maria-Luisa Ball Gown

2000

Bamboo Print Dress

Airplane Dress

Two-piece Slimline Suit

Galaxy Dress

Strapless Gown

Orange Suede and Paisley Ensemble

Hand-crafted Dress

Gothic Ensemble

Pierrot Ensemble

2010

White Dress

Coat Dress and Chaps

Planet Gaia

Jewel Tree Dress

Leather Tunic

Art Nouveau Gown

Cate Blanchett's Dress

Parka

Feather Dress

Bronze Dress

Animal Print Dress

Rosso Valentino Evening Dress

Belle Epoque Ensemble

White Shirt

Jumpsuit

Pastel Shell Ensemble

Embellished Tulle Dress

Asymmetric Dress

Denim Ensemble

Lace Dress

Ombré Dress

Striped Suit

Cutaway Top and Culottes

Organza Dress

Tea Dress

Ruffled Skirt

Structured Top and Skirt

LUXURY | FORM | EXOTICISM | ASCETICISM | SUBVERSION | UTILITY | EROTICISM | REVIVALISM | THEATRICAL | FUTURISM

INDEX

Bold type refers to illustrations

AUTHOR

MARNIE FOGG is a writer and previously a senior lecturer in fashion and textiles, with a master's degree in the theory and practice of art and design. Her previous publications explore topics such as fashion textiles, vintage fashion, illustration, and interiors. Titles include *Boutique: A '60s Cultural Phenomenon* (2003), *Couture Interiors: Living with Fashion* (2007), *Print in Fashion* (2006), *Vintage Knitwear* (2010), *The Fashion Design Directory* (2011), and *Fashion: The Whole Story* (2013).

PICTURE CREDITS

6–7 © Condé Nast Archive/Corbis **8** Rex Features **9–10** Catwalking **11** © Condé Nast Archive/Corbis **12** © Fairchild Photo Service/Condé Nast/Corbis **13** gorunway.com **16** The Metropolitan Museum of Art/Art Resource/Scala, Florence **18** Time & Life Pictures/Getty Images **19** AFP/Getty Images **20** Getty Images **22** Catwalking **24–25** Paul Cunningham/Corbis **26–27** WireImage/Getty Images **28** Catwalking **30** © YOAN VALAT/epa/Corbis **34** © Condé Nast Archive/Corbis **36** Rex Features **38** Gamma-Rapho/Getty Images **40** The Granger Collection/TopFoto **42** © ullsteinbild/TopFoto **43** Catwalking **44** Camera Press **46** Marcus Tondo/Gorunway/InDigitalteam **48–49** Yannis Vlamos/gorunway.com **52** Paul Poiret/V&A images **54–55** Getty Images **56** © Ted Spiegel/CORBIS **57** © Condé Nast Archive/Corbis **58** Catwalking **60** © Pierre Vauthey/Sygma/Corbis **62** Catwalking **64** © Fairchild Photo Service/Condé Nast/Corbis **66** Retna/Photoshot **67** AFP/Getty Images **70** © Condé Nast Archive/Corbis **72** Rei Kawakubo/V&A images **74** Carter Smith/Art + Commerce **76** © Fairchild Photo Service/Condé Nast/Corbis **78** Catwalking **80** Catwalking **82** Fairchild Photo Service/Condé Nast/Corbis **83** © 2013 Image copyright The Metropolitan Museum of Art/Art Resource/Scala, Florence **84** Catwalking **85** Jil Sander **88** André Durst © Vogue Paris **89** Gift of Mme. Elsa Schiaparelli, 1969/Bridgeman **90** © Bettmann/CORBIS **92** akg-images/Album/Warner Brothers **93** Collier Schorr/Art + Commerce **94** Getty Images **96–97** Catwalking **98** Charles Knight/Rex Features **99** © Sølve Sundsbø/Art + Commerce **100–101** Catwalking **102** Alexandro Garofalo/gorunway.com/InDigitalteam **106** © Hulton-Deutsch Collection/CORBIS **107** Harris & Ewing, Washington, D.C./Library of Congress **108** Hulton Collection/Getty Images **109** Getty Images **110–111** Pringle **112–113** SNAP/Rex Features **114** © Condé Nast Archive/Corbis **116** Michael Ochs Archives/Stringer/Getty Images **118** Craig McDean/Art + Commerce **120** Hendrik Ballhausen/dpa/Corbis **124–125** © Roger-Viollet/TopFoto **126–127** Getty Images **128** © Condé Nast Archive/Corbis **130** Photograph by Frederic Bukajlo/JDD/Gamma, Camera Press, London **131** © 2005 Credit: Topfoto/AP **132** Press Association **133** Rex Features **134** © Sølve Sundsbø/Art + Commerce **136** Firstview **138** Yannis Vlamos/gorunway.com **142** © Colin Jones/TopFoto **144** Gift of Barbara Hodes/FIT **145** © UPPA/Photoshot **146** Getty Images **148** © Sunset Boulevard/Corbis **149** Getty Images **150** AFP/Getty Images **152** Digital image copyright The Metropolitan Museum of Art/Art Resource/Scala, Florence **153** Digital Image Museum Associates/LACMA/Art Resource NY/Scala, Florence **154** Catwalking **156** Marcus Tondo/gorunway.com **157** © 2013 Image copyright The Metropolitan Museum of Art/Art Resource/Scala, Florence **160** © Bettmann/CORBIS 161 WARNER BROS./THE KOBAL COLLECTION **162** Ellen von Unwerth—Trunk **163** 2012 Getty Images **164** Craig McDean /Art + Commerce **166** Pedro Reguera **168** Marchesa **170–171** Catwalking **172** © Fairchild Photo Service/Condé Nast/Corbis **174** © Retna/Photoshot **178** Brian Duffy/Vogue © The Condé Nast Publications Ltd. **180** © Condé Nast Archive/Corbis **181** Paco Rabanne/V&A images **182** Time & Life Pictures/Getty Images **184** Gamma-Rapho via Getty Images **186** Camera Press **188** Iris van Herpen **192** Gorunway **194** Abbas/Magnum Photos